AF605555

Photo Credit: Ben Baker

Currently a presenter on Australia's beloved *Play School*, Rachael is an award-winning storyteller who has been writing, acting and producing for the screen and stage for over two decades. While storytelling is her career, Rachael's greatest passion is translating ancient wisdom in a way that speaks to everyone. Her previous books include a personal development guide, *Find Your Strength*, and a memoir, *Paris for Beginners*.

The Art of Forgiveness

The Art of Forgiveness

Rachael Coopes

First published in Australia in 2025 by Affirm Press,
a Simon & Schuster (Australia) Pty Limited company
Bunurong/Boon Wurrung Country
28 Thistlethwaite Street, South Melbourne VIC 3205

Affirm Press is located on the unceded land of the Bunurong/Boon Wurrung peoples of the Kulin Nation. Affirm Press pays respect to their Elders past and present.

New York Amsterdam/Antwerp London Toronto Sydney/Melbourne New Delhi
Visit our website at www.simonandschuster.com.au

AFFIRM PRESS and design are trademarks of Affirm Press Pty Ltd, Inc., used under licence by Simon & Schuster, LLC.

10 9 8 7 6 5 4 3 2 1

© Rachael Coopes 2025

All rights reserved. No part of this publication may be reproduced, stored in a retrieval system, or transmitted in any form or by any means, electronic, mechanical, photocopying, recording or otherwise, without prior permission of the publisher.

A Cataloguing-in-Publication entry for this book is available from the National Library of Australia

9781923135680 (hardback)

Cover design by Nada Backovic
Interior design by Steph Bishop-Hall
Typeset by J&M Typesetting in Garamond Premier Pro
Printed and bound in China by C&C Offset Printing Co., Ltd

This publication is meant as a source of valuable information, but it does not constitute individual psychological advice. Everyone's needs are different, and the author is not engaged in rendering professional services to the reader. Please reach out to a licensed mental health professional before adopting techniques described in this book, and especially if you are in crisis or distress.

For anyone who has ever tried to let go of something heavy to make their own journey lighter. For the voices in this book and all the wisdom they shared. And for Gabe, who has shown me the power of unconditional love.

Contents

INTRODUCTION

Life is a rich tapestry of experiences and emotions. We have our highs and lows, successes and failures, wins and losses. It is full of friendship and love, disappointments and betrayals. We forgive one another every day so our relationships, and society, can function. We do this in tiny ways, sometimes without even realising it, but there comes a day when something unforgivable happens and even the kindest, strongest and most open-minded of us can't move past it.

It is understandable, especially where a great injustice has occurred, a wrong has not been made right, or too much damage has been done. Feelings of anger, devastation and hatred towards others (or ourselves) consume us and become a giant obstacle to our future happiness. We are held down by the weight of resentment and reach a point where there is no way forward without facing it head-on. This can feel insurmountable, and no matter how hard we try, we can't just flick that switch to let it all go. So, we get stuck in this purgatory of un-forgivingness, unable to go back in time with Michael J Fox and his DeLorean to erase what has been done (only gen Xers will get that one). We see no conceivable way forward beyond our pain. How the hell do we 'just keep swimming', like little Dory in *Finding Nemo*? And what do we offer up in its place when forgiveness is not an option?

For those of you who are ready to move on but don't know how, this book will serve as an exploration of forgiveness, a trusted companion through an imperfect process, and the many ways we can approach it. It is not a how-to guide. The act of forgiving is not a simple one. It is complex and nuanced, and I guarantee it's not what most of us believe it to be. Through my journey in writing this book, I have discovered it is layered and contradictory and there are times when it's just not possible, or it looks very different to what we expected.

There is no one-size-fits-all. Forgiveness may not be the answer in situations and relationships where there has been extreme violence, abuse and trauma. I want to separate experiences with psychopaths and abusers, especially in cases that require specific and appropriate conversation, expertise, understanding and support. You will discover that discernment is key as you move through the research, stories and knowledge that many brave and generous people have shared with me.

Personally, I have found myself crippled by an inability to let go of regret, or someone's actions that caused immense suffering, and it definitely became a prison for me.

I have lived forgiveness in my own way. Growing up in the 1980s – a reckless, non-helicopter-parenting time – I was like a lot of gen Xers who pretty much parented themselves. I spent my childhood between two houses, my primary one a vibrant apartment with a struggling, twenty-year-old single mum trying to survive and do her best. She was a baby herself, trying to figure everything out, working her booty off, bringing herself up as well as me. She was doing all the normal twenty-year-old things, like dating ratbags, partying and hanging out with friends, while adulting hard by keeping a roof over our heads and food on the table. On weekends, I headed an hour west of Sydney, far from friends and the familiar, to stay at Dad's. I'd look forward to it all week, but then, feeling like a guest, I'd cry to Mum on the phone and ask her to bring me home.

There was no way I was going to repeat history and watch my kids schlep between bases, with all the physical and emotional baggage that goes with them on a weekly basis. And as much as I loved the closeness Mum and I had that I didn't see in other families, I wanted a solid unit for my kids one day.

I was thirty-eight when I had my son, G. Mum had always worried I'd 'miss the boat', but when I did get my ticket on the pregnancy cruise, I hit some rough conditions and ended up shipwrecked. The fear of choosing the wrong partner, and ending up a single parent, had plagued me since I was young. I'm convinced it was a huge block in my relationships; I was searching for some unattainable situation that was one hundred per cent unbreakable.

When I broke up with my long-term partner in my early thirties, I met mum for coffee. I needed some maternal love, someone who would tell me I had loads of time, all would be well, I'd meet the right person at the right time and I would not end up dying alone.

'I don't know if I'm ever going to feel like that again,' I confessed. 'Maybe that's it. Maybe I'm meant to be alone.'

Pragmatic as ever, but with dancing eyes, she offered up: 'Well, this might cheer you up. I thought as an early birthday present I would freeze your eggs.'

This didn't make me feel better, but it did momentarily shift my anger to a new target, which was a welcome respite from wallowing in heartbreak.

I didn't take her up on the frozen eggs, but I did set my sights on an imperfect relationship – and I found one. It was fast and furious and messier than any relationship I'd been in, but trying to choose safety had failed me until now and I would make this one work! I would ride the tempest waves and get seaworthy.

And then I found myself pregnant, separated, facing the very future I had spent my whole life avoiding. The years of working hard to protect myself, and my family, from this scenario, were all for nothing. I had made my bed and now I had to lie in it, but more infuriatingly, so did my son. Something broke in me through that process. Something irreparable. And though the journey of forgiving myself, and G's dad, has been messy, long and complicated, it's been an incredibly rewarding one. And still, I know that the voyage isn't over yet.

Having dedicated my life to storytelling, yoga and mindfulness, my imposter syndrome voice has often been deafening and I feel like a fraud whenever I'm not practising what I preach. This, along with my impeccable teachers, has given me great accountability. They inspire me to search for what gets in the way of my ability to move towards a more integrated and peaceful state of being, to live with integrity, and to work with my aversion to those who trigger or hurt me. But it feels like a never-ending story, an unreachable state of being, with no happily-ever-after ending in sight, just a constant work in progress.

Eleven years ago, when I found myself juggling work, exhaustion, a baby with reflux and a bitter separation, I was in a deep hole of grief and anger. But I knew I didn't want to be a victim of circumstance or blame anyone else for my choices. I couldn't picture how I'd forge a happy future for my son and myself. Having decades of yoga, mindfulness and meditation practice under my belt, I had many tools I could apply to my life, which were fundamental in keeping my head above water. Let me tell you, it would not have been pretty without them. But even with all of those in place, I still couldn't see a way forward. And so I made it my mission to do whatever it took, to move beyond fear and fury into our future.

Not only have I experienced my own relationship breakdowns and betrayals, but I've also watched ugly divorces, business partners falling out, and family members and friends causing one another endless pain, wasting decades of their lives. I have seen too many people destroy themselves, and others, in the name of punishment and vindication, and countless others beating themselves up for a wrong path taken or missed opportunity. And so, I started to think a lot about forgiveness, and how the hell you practise it when it feels impossible.

My strength lies in synthesising vast and complex subjects and making them engaging and accessible. Within these pages, I have endeavoured to do this with a thorny subject we all grapple with. I have compiled existing wisdom, knowledge and perspectives in a way that will make it possible for you to pull them into your own life and move forward.

I share principles from philosophies I have been steeped in since I was eighteen years old. My frame carried a light thirty-seven kilos and a hefty mountain of mental health baggage when I found myself sitting in a psychiatrist's office. He gave me a bunch of books on ancient practices like Buddhism and yoga and sent me off on a lifelong love affair with them. This began my journey as a dedicated student of the ancient wisdom of the yogis. I will share much of the knowledge that has been helpful for me and my students. None of it is new and none of it comes from me. But I have completed thousands of hours of formal and informal training, workshops and study, and I have had masterful teachers who cultivated my understanding. To this day, I study and embody it daily with the same enthusiasm and discipline of my early years. And for the past two decades, I have worked professionally as a yoga teacher, trainer and mindfulness educator in studios, organisations and institutions of all sizes, and shared my knowledge through storytelling in magazines and books.

In addition to yoga and mindfulness, I will explore many other ancient philosophies that provide similar insight, including Stoicism, Greek and Celtic mythology, Indigenous wisdom and traditional Chinese medicine. These practices provide profound knowledge that has stood the test of time. We will also look at the etymology of the word 'forgiveness' and how it has changed across different eras, cultures and religions. From this place, I will connect some dots between the old and new and provide contemporary ways to apply and use them today.

But you won't just be listening to me bang on about the power of forgiveness. You'll hear suggestions and personal stories from a range of experts and brave souls who have worked with forgiveness in their own lives and helped others practise it. We will look at what recent scientific and academic research says about forgiveness, especially around neuroscience and health, and explore what psychology offers in the way of theories, frameworks and tools. Using past and present practices, I'll weave together a multifaceted tapestry of what forgiveness can look like and how we can work with it. It's by no means an exhaustive list. Instead, it is a collection of some of the most powerful perspectives and insights I encountered in my journey.

Based on this collective wisdom, I'll share exercises and suggestions you can use both now and in the future. It is a lifetime practice you can revisit in new ways, time and time again. This will be your practical guide for contemplation and action. I've done my best to dilute some pretty strong cocktails into light aperitifs.

At the end of the pandemic, I found myself in an unrecognisable and fragmented world, where friendships ended over vaccine mandates and conspiracy theories. Fundamentalism and popularism were on the rise and politics were more polarised than ever. The division and hatred within communities, once deeply bonded and connected, was heartbreaking to witness. Friends I'd known for decades were not talking to one another and their coldness towards each other was icier than the Arctic. It felt like we were all on the Titanic, waiting for it to hit that final iceberg. The dissonance has gotten worse since then, with two international wars threatening the modern world, and a crash seems more imminent than ever. It's like we are holding our breath in the bitter wilderness, waiting for that final, icy thump. These were some of the driving forces for writing this book.

Another force was my eternal curiosity which is always searching for answers to life's big questions. What I really gained through the process though, was more questions. This reminds me of the first time I sat with my Sanskrit teacher, Manorama (Ma) D'Alvia. There were about two hundred of us, eager yogis from all over the world, doing our yoga teacher training at the Omega Institute for Holistic Studies in New York State. We had been practising, meditating and sitting on the floor for 12–13 hours a day. Our bodies and brains were tired and full. But as soon as Ma spoke, we were hungry again, wanting to drink in all the wisdom she was willing to share. I was a meerkat, taking it all in, not wanting to miss a thing. I fought my impulse to put my hand up; I was bursting to the seams with questions. Despite myself, my meerkat paw shot up, and I machine-gunned a few of my most pressing queries. Sitting upright, a shawl wrapped around her shoulders, dark hair and eyes silently regarding me for what seemed like an awfully long time, she smiled and said: 'There is no wisdom in the answers, only the questions.'

The process of writing this book has been exactly that. The deeper I went down the rabbit hole of research, and listening to stories, the more I heard Ma's voice in my head. There is no direct answer to the question 'what is forgiveness?' Just as there is no direct answer to the question 'what is love?' What I am one hundred per cent certain of is this: there is enormous wisdom and reward in practising the art of forgiveness. In a world as fractured and uncertain as the one we find ourselves in now, contemplating forgiveness, and how we can foster more of it in our lives, can only build a better future for ourselves and those around us. Everyone I interviewed and spoke to during the process thanked me for the journey they took while contemplating our conversations. There's something magic that happens when we plunge into the heart, and the art, of forgiveness. So, dive deep, swim far and come up for air when you need to.

I promise you'll return, lighter, freer and ready to rumble into your next chapter.

And if anything doesn't land, it just means my synthesis isn't quite there. Anything that provides you with any kind of insight and practical ways to move forward is thanks to the amazing teachers I've had and the generous souls who shared their perspectives for this book.

There are many great figures in history who had every reason to hate, and yet they preached forgiveness. After being imprisoned in South Africa for twenty-seven years for opposing apartheid, it would be understandable if Nelson Mandela spent the remainder of his life holding a grudge against all those responsible for his incarceration. But the message he imparted on his release was not one of revenge or vindication. It was about leaving the past behind: 'As I walked out the door toward the gate that would lead to my freedom, I knew if I didn't leave my bitterness and hatred behind, I'd still be in prison.'

When the greatest minds of our age speak of forgiveness so often, surely it is a call to pay attention. When it is so intricately linked to our freedom, perhaps it is a priority, not an option, to get more forgiveness in our lives – whatever that means – starting now.

WHY FORGIVE?

From ancient Greek mythology to modern neuroscience, the message is clear: there is much to lose when we don't forgive and everything to gain when we do. The price may be too high when we put our heads in the sand, ostrich-like, and avoid the courageous path of forgiveness.

When Agamemnon, the Greek mythological king of Argos, set off with his army to fight the Trojan War, he couldn't possibly have imagined the series of events that would unfold because of one unforgiving moment. In the same way, none of us ever really knows the impact of our actions or the consequences of the choices we make at the time.

Agamemnon was sailing to the aid of his brother, Menelaus, who couldn't forgive his wife, Helen (Zeus's daughter, who happened to be the most beautiful woman in the world), for running off with Paris, a Trojan prince. Artemis, who had a grudge against Agamemnon for killing a sacred deer on her land, refused to provide the winds he needed to set sail. The only way he could move forward was by sacrificing his daughter, Iphigenia, and so he did.

When Agamemnon's wife, Clytemnestra, found out, she was full of grief and rage. The Trojan war was not resolved quickly, as wars never are, and so it dragged on for many years. In that time, Clytemnestra's fury grew, and she took a lover, Aegisthus, Agamemnon's cousin. This was payback as the cousins had their own bad blood. Agamemnon's dad, Atreus, had cooked Aegisthus' brothers and fed them to their own dad, Thyestes, in revenge for stealing his wife. As the saying goes, you can choose your friends, but you can't choose your family.

Meanwhile, in the warring city of Troy, the seer Cassandra had prophesied the Trojans' impending doom. Despite her forewarnings, they welcomed beautiful Helen to the city, which kicked off the whole sordid affair, and brought in the infamous Trojan horse, which she told them was full of hidden Greek warriors. When the Greek ambush was victorious, Cassandra was taken prisoner, a spoil of war.

On Agamemnon's triumphant return to Argos, vengeful lovers Clytemnestra and Aegisthus killed both Agamemnon and the long-suffering Cassandra (who, by the way, had also foreseen their fates, but of course, no one listens to the 'crazy' lady who seems to be smarter and know more than everyone else).

Agamemnon's daughter Electra and son Orestes were devastated by his murder and planned to get their own payback. Although hesitating momentarily as his mum begged him for mercy, Orestes did wreak his vengeance on both Aegisthus and Clytemnestra, repaying the debt of his father's life.

But it doesn't end there! Because this is a Greek tragedy where no one forgives, and everyone loses. In true Greek myth form, the powerful Furies enter stage right, the three goddesses of vengeance and retribution, sent from above to punish those who commit crimes against the natural order. The Furies descend upon Orestes for violating the sanctified relationship between mother and son and endlessly torment him into madness. And no one lived happily ever after. The end.

This, my friends, is Greek mythology, where so many of the narratives illustrate how every act of vengeance leads to more destruction. In the story of Agamemnon, the Furies ensure that even justified situations of unforgiveness and payback don't escape divine punishment.

Since the beginning of time, tales of revenge reign supreme over those of forgiveness. Kissing and making up doesn't make for good drama. What does is pitting good against bad, the dark side opposite Jedi goodness, Darth Vader and Luke, Iron Man and Thanos, Daenerys and Cersei, arch enemies in an eternal showdown, creating epic CGI battle scenes that satiate our overstimulated, highly distractable modern minds.

But the endgame is still the same. The cost of our grudges, rightness and vindication is not cheap, even if we have all the justification in the world for our vengeance. Neuroscience agrees that by holding onto our hatred, we are handing over our physical and mental health, and so the cycle of destruction goes on.

BORN THIS WAY

I'm a Taurus. We get a bad rap for being stubborn little grudge-holders. I prefer to see it as holding true to our values, which the Stoics would say is the most important thing to do, and we will cover that in the next chapter. We are not quick to temper, us bulls. We are happy chilling in the paddock with our food and friends until some annoying, overdressed Spaniard with a ridiculous hat enters and starts waving a red flag around. Even then, we will ignore them prancing in their sparkly tight pants. But if they start poking us with those lances, then it's game on, and you don't want to be in the pathway of a charging bull. And once we've charged, we are never letting go of that hatred for red flags, or Spanish men in boleros.

If you are not a Taurus, but you feel like you have always found it harder than other people to give up a grudge, it may just be the structure of your brain, or genetics. Differing structural brain anatomy suggests that forgiveness could be a trait people are born with. Commonwealth Professor Emeritus Everett Worthington dedicated his career to studying forgiveness. His research found that some people are naturally more forgiving, and those who are, have higher levels of agreeableness and lower levels of neuroticism. They tend to be more satisfied with their lives and have less depression, anxiety, stress, anger and hostility. While those who tend to ruminate are more likely to hold onto grudges and are therefore less likely to forgive. The ruminators are more likely to experience severe depression and posttraumatic stress disorder, as well as other health conditions.

Even if you are born to be less forgiving than others, it doesn't mean you have to remain that way, bulls charging at every flag you see being waved. Differences in metabolic brain activity associated with the inclination to forgive may mean that this trait could be altered throughout life. Influences like life experiences with trustworthy people or the opposite – betrayal – can set the stage for how much a person tends to forgive. This should foster our compassion for those who have a long run of bad luck, making it harder for them to reframe and move on. Life encounters can make you a charging, or chilling, bull.

THE DOMINO EFFECT

When we don't forgive others, we find ourselves in a state of resentment, which creates a neurological and physical domino effect, just like it did for Agamemnon. Each time we remember the injustice, anger triggers the stress response, causing the body to prioritise systems only related to immediate survival and suppress the immune system. The mind races so you can make quick decisions and focus on the perceived threat, which is useful from an evolutionary perspective when an actual tiger is running towards you.

In the case of grudges, the tiger is normally your feelings towards those who have harmed you in the past. The immediate threat is long gone, but the damage feels just as present and worse than anything a tiger could manage. When we don't let go, we keep cycling back, reliving the emotions. The threat state keeps getting triggered and suppresses the immune system again and again. In moments of crisis, for the short term, this is necessary. However, when we do it consistently, over a long period of time, our health will eventually suffer. Not forgiving others isn't punishing *them*, it's making *us* sick.

THE LIMBIC SYSTEM

To understand how this domino effect happens, the brain's emotional processing area, the limbic system, takes centre stage. Inside this structure is a little section called the nucleus accumbens, which sends happy chemicals through the brain when we experience something pleasant. Conversely, when we experience something unpleasant, like the negative feelings associated with not forgiving, a tiny but powerful part of the brain, the amygdala, sends not-so-happy signals to the nucleus accumbens.

The amygdala is a little guy with a big job, controlling

our fight-or-flight centre. When we ruminate over how someone has harmed us, or how we messed up, the amygdala gets very trigger-happy. It's like pressing a button, over and over, stimulating the nucleus accumbens to elicit pain sensors in the brain. This delivers negative chemicals while diminishing the happy ones like serotonin and dopamine. It's akin to lab rats in a cage, pressing a lever over and over to get a drink, but instead of receiving sugar water, they receive a toxic substance. Over time, as that button keeps getting pressed, the amygdala becomes more sensitive, and the rumination reinforces this destructive pattern. A study by Yoav Litvin and colleagues from Donald Pfaff's Laboratory of Neurobiology and Behavior at Rockerfeller University illustrated how this continuous rumination on negative thoughts gets hardwired into our brains. Their experiment with laboratory mice showed that when a mouse is repeatedly bullied, it stops doing normal mouse things, its brain chemistry is altered, it suffers from anxiety and stays in a frozen 'fight-or-flight' state long after the bully is removed. According to an Italian study by Pietro Pietrini and colleagues from the Clinical Psychology Branch at the University of Pisa Medical School using MRI imaging of the brain, this chronic emotional distress may lead to clinical conditions like depression.

Rumination erodes not just mental, but physical health. It alters cardiovascular reactivity, reduces sleep quality, and stimulates the production of stress hormones such as cortisol. When triggered, the amygdala sends stress messages to the hypothalamus, which is the command centre for the rest of the body via the autonomic nervous system. The autonomic nervous system controls things like breathing, blood pressure, heartbeat, dilation of blood vessels and the airways of the lungs. The nervous system can either be in a sympathetic 'fight-or-flight state', which is all-systems-alert, or a parasympathetic 'rest-and-digest' state, which is all cool-calm-collected. When the hypothalamus triggers the fight-or-flight state, Howard LeWine, Chief Medical Editor at Harvard Health Publishing, explains that it sends signals to the adrenal glands, which pump the hormone epinephrine (most of us know it as adrenaline) into the bloodstream, bringing on a bunch of physiological changes. The heart beats faster, pulse rate and blood pressure rise, breathing becomes more rapid, the small airways of the lungs open wide, senses become sharper and blood sugar is released. In turn, this triggers other stress hormones, including cortisol, which can wreak havoc on the body. Especially when there is chronic, ongoing activation of what is meant to be a short-term survival response.

THE COST OF GETTING STUCK

The American Psychological Association says that repeated, long-term activation of the fight-or-flight response and associated stress hormones affect almost all the body's processes, including the musculoskeletal, respiratory, cardiovascular, endocrine, gastrointestinal, nervous and reproductive systems.

Consultant psychiatrist Sami Ouanes and psychiatrist and professor for geriatric psychiatry, Julius Popp, reviewed the existing body of evidence on the interrelationships between cortisol, cognitive impairment and Alzheimer's disease. In their research they confirmed that prolonged elevation of our stressy friend cortisol takes quite a toll on the body and mind. Because cortisol shrinks the hippocampus, the memory centre of the brain, it can reduce our cognitive and executive functioning, language, processing speed and memory – among other things. So impactful is the long-term elevation of cortisol on memory, it may put you at higher risk of dementia, especially if you suffer from PTSD.

Researchers at the University College of London reviewed and quantified the risk of future dementia associated with PTSD across populations and published their findings in the *British Journal of Psychology*. They found that PTSD is associated with a significant risk of dementia, attesting to the impact of the stress response on the brain, memory and cognitive decline.

In addition, the Framingham Heart Study confirmed in their research that elevated cortisol not only impacts cognitive performance and memory, but brain volume. Higher cortisol is associated with lower brain volume. And due to the connection between the brain and the immune system, science writer Agnese Mariotti expounds that chronic stress can trigger diseases linked to inflammation, including cardiovascular dysfunctions, diabetes, cancer, autoimmune syndromes and several mental illnesses.

So while we are holding on to distressing memories, stewing away on bitterness, refusing to forgive, our body and mind are paying the ultimate price.

KANGAROOS IN HEADLIGHTS

I spent some time working in the Northern Territory where there are long stretches of roads with unbounded speed limits and bounding kangaroos. In the evening, those dark roads – with no streetlights, just bushland blanketed in black – are particularly fraught for drivers. One night, I came heart-stoppingly close to ending both a kangaroo's life and my own. Driving home after a soul-nourishing campfire yarn with beloved friends and their kids, a giant, muscular grey creature appeared in front of the car, seemingly out of nowhere. I slammed on the brakes, and in slow motion I slid towards him, somehow veering left enough, without losing control of the car completely. (I say he because he was a leviathan, and male kangaroos up north tend to be much larger than their female counterparts.) I ran off the road, fortunately not into the ghost-like gums that now appeared in my path. I was breathless, shaking, all the potent chemicals flooding my body, probably saving both of our lives with their quick physiological prowess. He just stood there for an age, hypnotically frozen in time. It was only when another kangaroo leapt past that, just like a switch being flicked, he was off, bounding back into the black wilderness.

HARDWIRING THE BRAIN – FROZEN CIRCUITS

During my meditation study with Ayurvedic pioneer and Vedic scholar Mother Maya (Maya Tiwari), she would say, 'pain is normal, hurt is not'. In other words, we are going to experience loss and pain as part of this human experience; that's the deal of being alive. But when we keep reliving that suffering, we move to a more permanent state of hurt, which doesn't have to be part of the deal.

Scientist, teacher, lecturer and author Dr Joe Dispenza also talks about this 'roo-in-headlights 'stuckness' of the mind in the context of frozen circuits. He says our brains' circuits get hardwired by our minds circling back to the same things. The more we experience it, the more we solidify those feelings in the brain, until that frozen condition becomes our new norm. Neuroscientists commonly call the brain an 'anticipation machine'. It's like we are armed and ready for the next experience based on what's happened to us before.

It's important to acknowledge what happens to us in each moment, to feel all the feelings that arise and not ignore them. Mindfulness and psychology practices focus a lot on this. When we do it mindfully, in meditation or therapy, for example, it can help us in the process of letting them go.

However, what the neuroscience and meditation experts are saying is that by *not* forgiving, we re-enforce and amplify feelings of hostility, creating a state of stuckness that is challenging to extract ourselves from. Fixating on negative feelings, coming back to them again and again, and not having any separation from them keeps us in fight-or-flight mode. The longer we ruminate, the more we are likely to hardwire pain into our brain and, ultimately, into our bodies, in the form of disease. Or as a psychologist once said to me when my bulimia became life-threatening many years ago, it's not a 'disease'; it's 'dis-ease'. When we are not at ease in our bodies and minds, sometimes for extended periods of time, we may experience disease. Understanding how to break the circuit of that hardwiring and feel more at ease is critical in moving towards forgiveness.

THE DOLLARS AND SENSE OF NOT FORGIVING

I've known family lawyer Sarah Swan since we were young, but we connected over our Saturday morning chats post-yoga, which I taught in Bondi for years. Her brother has been a close friend of mine since we were fifteen and the family have been a part of my life across many chapters. Sarah has this incredible combination of all the smarts and steadiness a lawyer needs and the adventurous, curious heart of a yogi.

Having seen the actual cost of divorce, she tells me it's not only the buckets of money that people lose but years of their lives. Sometimes their whole lives. And the people who really pay the price are the ones they least want to hurt – their kids.

Sarah believes that the underlying reasons that cause resentment, such as lack of forgiveness, cannot be resolved in court. People go through this enormous, time-consuming process that absorbs all their time and energy, and even if they get everything they want in court, they feel empty. It's a let-down. They don't feel like there has been any justice. If they haven't forgiven what is sitting beneath their anger, which generally has nothing to do with what's being decided in court, they wind up exactly where they began at the beginning of the process. They get stuck; they never move on with their lives.

In addition, despite parents' efforts to hide their

feelings, children are usually aware when there's bitterness between them. Sarah says: 'Kids are the ones who ultimately pay the highest price for their parents not forgiving. They didn't choose to be born. Their parents made that choice, likely out of love for one another at some point. And it's not their fault these two adults can't stand each other anymore.'

WHAT HAPPENS WHEN WE FORGIVE

When we consciously move away from anger towards forgiveness, we are the champions, my friends. There is substantial evidence that forgiveness provides many physical and psychological benefits, and the 2015 book by David R Williams, Everett Worthington and Loren Toussaint *Forgiveness and Health* analyses much of it. It suggests forgiveness may lower blood pressure, improve cardiovascular health, boost the immune system, reduce chronic pain and lead to better sleep quality. Psychologically, it says, it can reduce anxiety, depression and anger (fostering emotional healing), enhance emotional well-being and psychological resilience, increase self-esteem, and strengthen relationships by promoting trust and empathy. According to the American

Psychological Association, forgiveness is even linked to lower mortality rates. Simply thinking about forgiving an offender was shown to improve people's cardiovascular and nervous systems in one of the earliest studies on forgiveness in 2001.

Maybe that's the first step of letting go of our hatred and getting our health and well-being back. We simply open ourselves up to the possibility of forgiving. Rather than setting sail for war like a Greek mythological king, contemplating forgiveness may well be the more heroic act.

WHY FORGIVE: A SUMMARY

- Greek mythology tells us that no one wins when we seek revenge or don't forgive.
- While some of us are wired to hold a grudge, it doesn't mean we can't change.
- Resentment may create a domino effect, triggering the autonomic nervous system's fight-or-flight state.
- The amygdala can become more sensitive each time we trigger that state, amplifying emotions.
- The cocktail of hormones that flood the body during this state creates mental and physiological changes that

can impact almost all the body's processes.

- When we get stuck like 'roos in rumination headlights, hardwiring our frozen circuits over long periods of time, it can affect our physical and mental health.
- From the Battle of Troy to the family law courts of today, the cost of not forgiving is too high a price to pay – for everyone involved.
- When we do forgive, we are happier and healthier.

OPEN AWARENESS MEDITATION

Drawn from open awareness meditation, this practice allows us to experience everything as new and changing. It lets thoughts arise, gives us some separation from the emotion attached, and interrupts the circuit.

EXERCISE

Sit down in a comfortable place and start by listening to the sounds around you. See if you can drop the separation between 'you' and 'listening'. As you notice thoughts arise, let them bubble up and then, importantly, let them float away. Expand your awareness to feel the air around you, the temperature, the breath, physical sensations, smells, taste, everything.
As thoughts and feelings come up, feel them. Rest in the awareness of holding them and letting them melt away, as they naturally will.

ETYMOLOGY

TOXIC POSITIVITY

In the LEGO films, our hero is Emmet, the happy-go-lucky master builder and construction worker. He loves everything and everyone and has an ever-positive mindset, no matter the circumstance. His catchy theme song, 'Everything is Awesome', is the perfect toxic positivity anthem. Emmet's journey through the film is to recognise that the world is not uniformly awesome, that it's a complex and colourful place, full of darkness and light and everything in between. He leaves his ordered world to embrace the idea that individual creativity should be welcomed, in all its glorious messiness.

In the same way, it's not until we face our own experience with brutal honesty, and ditch the 'Everything is Awesome' mantra, that we can find real joy. Toxic positivity is the understanding that no matter how negative our feelings, or how dire our situation, we must maintain a positive mindset. This involves denying feelings like anger, fear, disappointment and those we deem 'bad' that get in the way of forgiving and forgetting. By pushing away and avoiding uncomfortable feelings, we bypass how we are really processing the world around us, we don't validate our emotional reality, and we live in a state of denial.

DENIAL

According to the *Merriam-Webster Dictionary*, denial is a 'defence mechanism in which confrontation with a personal problem, or with reality, is avoided by denying the existence of the problem or reality'. It was first researched by Anna Freud, the daughter of infamous Austrian neurologist and founder of psychoanalysis Sigmund Freud. Anna was a prolific writer and highly accomplished psychoanalyst in her own right. In her book, *The Ego and the Mechanisms of Defence*, she suggested that denial is an unconscious strategy that prevents us from feeling anxiety and distress. It protects the ego from discomfort when we can't cope or when things feel like they're too much to handle. Although some of Anna's work has been rejected or disproven over time, her ideas on defence mechanisms and denial are still widely accepted by many psychologists today.

Research has shown the suppression of, or inability to express, negative feelings such as sadness, disappointment and anger can have dire consequences for our well-being, even increasing the risk of dying earlier. In the book *Emotional Expression and Health* Ivan Nyklicek, Lydia Temoshok and Ad Vingerhoets reviewed the extensive literature on emotions and cardiovascular disease, ascertaining that suppressing our emotions increases stress levels, which in turn negatively impacts our health. Nicole Roberts from Arizona State University confirmed via her research with colleagues that emotional suppression is associated with increased cardiovascular activation and blood pressure. Another study led by Thomas Beblo of the Clinic of Psychiatry and Psychotherapy at the University of Bielefeld, Germany found that suppression of emotions correlated to depressive symptoms. While psychiatrist Benjamin Chapman, Associate Professor at the University of Rochester Medical Center examined the association between suppression and all-cause cardiovascular and cancer mortality, over twelve years of follow up, and observed there was a significant link. Higher emotional suppression leads to higher mortality rates. Ignoring emotions dismisses our reality as we desperately try to get rid of those icky feelings.

In Disney Pixar's animated film *Inside Out 2*, we see the well-intentioned character Joy, who is in the driver's seat of our heroine Riley's brain, shooting all the unwanted experiences and memories into a big dumpster pile in the back of Riley's mental storage space. Much of the film is the journey of Joy understanding that Riley needs all her memories, and that we all need to experience every emotion, positive or negative, for our personal growth. Accepting undesirable feelings in the short term tends to be more beneficial to our development and mental and physical health in the long run.

Forgiveness is not bypassing your emotional reality, gaslighting yourself into a false positive unreality. It doesn't deny or throw away what has happened to you or how it made you feel. But it may be the key to moving towards a truly positive future.

As Buddhist monk, writer and meditation teacher Jack Kornfield says: 'Forgiveness does not ignore the truth of our suffering. Forgiveness is not weak. It demands courage and integrity. Yet only forgiveness and love can bring about the peace we long for.'

LETTING OURSELVES OFF THE HOOK

From a psychological perspective, forgiveness is not ignoring our feelings, condoning someone's behaviour towards us or reconciling with someone who caused us harm. It is not accepting abuse or staying in a toxic situation. It is not making amends or kissing and making up. It doesn't mean there's no personal, financial or legal accountability. It's not necessarily about us holding positive feelings towards those who hurt us. It's about letting go of the destructive negative thoughts we have towards them.

Some of those things may happen, and compassion, or acceptance, may be helpful in the process of forgiving. But ultimately, forgiveness is not about anyone else. It is the radical act of taking ownership of how we move forward, whatever has happened to us in the past. We may have no part in the situation that has caused resentment. We may be victims of things beyond our control. But it is our responsibility to ourselves to resolve it in some way for our own brighter future.

Many of us think it means letting others off the hook for their negative actions. Because of this misunderstanding, we believe that it is somehow condoning their behaviour, so they get off scot-free. But as we examine the roots of the word and explore some personal stories, you will discover that it is ourselves we let off the hook, not the people who caused us suffering.

As the famous Alcoholics Anonymous quote goes, 'Resentment is like drinking poison and waiting for the other person to die.'

THE ART OF ...

Is there anything more wonderfully subjective than art? One of my favourite images is the duck-rabbit illusion, which has been dividing viewers since the 1890s. In the ambiguous picture, some people see a duck while others see a rabbit. Of course, the truth is that it is both and neither. When you really strip it back, we may all see something different in the image itself, but it's simply lines on a page. As Anaïs Nin said in her 1961 autobiographical novel *Seduction of the Minotaur*: 'We don't see things as they are, we see them as we are.' Subjectivity is based on our personal experience and feelings, rather than facts.

The art of doing something can be understood in a few ways. It incorporates the idea of gaining a skill through experience, study or observation, and then combining it with our subjective imagination. We can diligently wade through the research and philosophy, but then it's up to us to integrate and process it in our own way. This liberates us from the shackles of rigidity because although there is a mindful and disciplined head-based approach, our creativity will determine our heart-based relationship to whatever it is we are doing.

The art of forgiveness looks at this messy subject from an ordered, cerebral place while inviting ingenuity and vision in forging our own path forward. As you observe how forgiveness plays out in your life, skill will meet your imagination.

SO WHAT THE HELL IS FORGIVENESS ANYWAY?

When we examine the etymology of the word forgiveness, some key things stand out. As I mentioned earlier, it's not about letting other people off the hook. Rather, it's about letting ourselves off the hook.

According to the *American Heritage Dictionary*, the word 'forgive' comes from the Old English 'giefan' and 'forgiefan'. 'Giefen' is to give, while 'forgiefan' means to give, leave off (anger), remit (a debt), but also to give up. It originates from the Indo-European root 'ghabh', which is to give or receive. Similarly, the Latin word, 'perdonare' (where our English word 'pardon' comes from), means to give wholeheartedly, without reservation.

The roots of forgiving therefore centre around the two actions – giving and giving up. But there is also this idea of receiving. From an etymological perspective, the question is: what do you need to give, and give up, in the process of forgiveness? And what do you receive when we you forgive?

The current understanding we have of forgiveness comes from the Bible, which uses three Greek verbs connected to this notion of giving up. They centre around the idea of cancelling a debt and letting go but with something even greater – mercy, which we will be discussing later.

GIVING UP VS GRACE

According to the *Oxford English Dictionary*, to forgive is: 'to give up resentment against, pardon (an offender)'. This concept of pardoning, or cancelling an offence, is inherited from Biblical times, so in this context, the idea of wrongdoing is closely related to the concept of sin.

The notion of cancelling an offence comes from three Greek verbs that appear in the Bible, two of which are almost synonyms. 'Aphiemi' means to take away or cancel.

Rather than overlooking any wrongdoing, it's as if it had never even happened. You let it go and never speak of it again. 'Apoluw' means to dissolve, to release, like aphiemi, but it's more about letting go or freeing someone from a debt. The whole premise of confession is based on the understanding that God is always willing to wipe the slate clean.

There is a third verb used in the context of forgiveness – 'kharizomai' or 'charizomai' – which is a little different. Derived from 'charis', which means grace, it is to show compassion or kindness. There's an element of mercy in the meaning that goes beyond simply overlooking someone's misconduct.

It is one thing to let go of someone's transgression, to release them from owing us anything and move on with our lives. But it is another to show benevolence towards them, to wish happiness towards someone who has wronged us. That requires a whole lot of Zen, Teflon and magical powers most of us just don't have.

In the parable of the prodigal son, a young man boldly asks for his inheritance and then predictably wastes it living his best life. When he returns home, his head not held high, rather than his father losing his temper and teaching him a lesson, he welcomes him with open arms. The prodigal son's older brother is understandably miffed, having done the right thing by staying home and working hard. His father insists that they must celebrate because someone in their family was lost but has now been found. The parable demonstrates the importance of welcoming those who make mistakes, erasing a debt and showing grace.

The ultimate example of forgiveness, however, is Jesus sacrificing his life so that imperfect mortals could receive mercy from God. And in his final moments on the cross, he calls out to God, asking him to forgive his executioners: 'Father, forgive them, for they do not know what they are doing.'

The Stoics, however, viewed forgiveness in a very different way. In fact, some may argue that they didn't believe in forgiveness at all.

HOLDING ON TO WHO YOU ARE

Stoicism was hugely popular in ancient Greece and Rome. A school of Hellenic philosophy that started around 300 BCE after Alexander the Great's death, it held that virtue was the key to a life well lived. Because of this, the Stoics viewed forgiveness through a very different lens.

When we look at Socrates, for example, there is an assertion that we should not cause harm or return evil for evil. Rather, no matter how someone else acts, we should respond from a place of virtue and maintain a disposition of benevolence towards them, whether they are a friend or enemy. There's no mercy, just a focus on maintaining our own values through every altercation.

Socrates was well known for questioning the status quo and the existing understanding of justice at the time. As a result, he was imprisoned for impiety and corrupting the youth of the day. During his captivity, he was composed and kind to his guards. He didn't blame them, as they were not responsible for his incarceration; they were just doing their jobs. But he also didn't hold resentment towards the people who were culpable for his imprisonment. He focused his efforts on preserving his character and how he held himself throughout the whole affair, ensuring he did no injustice. This even included refusing to escape his execution, which his old friend Crito had arranged but Socrates declined, as it was not the right thing to do.

This is the biggest difference between a Christian interpretation of forgiveness and a Stoic one. In Stoicism, the emphasis is more on forgivingness rather than forgiveness.

Socrates remains calm, doesn't cancel the debt of those who wronged him, but instead focuses on holding on to his values. From the Stoic perspective, staying true to yourself and holding on to who you are, no matter what someone else has done, is more important than anything else.

MODERN DEFINITIONS

The *Cambridge Dictionary* defines forgiveness as follows: 'To stop blaming or being angry with someone for something that person has done, or not punish them for something.' The *Merriam-Webster Dictionary* says: 'To cease to feel resentment against.'

These modern definitions emphasise ceasing and stopping. In other words, halting the feelings of blame and anger that we have had towards someone. We're not pardoning them, showing mercy, focusing on our virtue or letting them off the hook. We simply stop our part in the dynamic. We stop punishing them and let go of our negative emotions. We break the circuit and let our 'roos stuck in headlights leap happily into the wilderness.

The good news (or bad news, depending on how you perceive it) is that this approach to forgiveness empowers us to act without anyone else needing to be part of the process. That gives us agency and puts us in the driver's seat, despite what someone else does or doesn't do. From this perspective, no matter the circumstances, we get to decide how that process of letting go, giving or giving up, erasing a debt or stopping the circuit will operate in our lives – and what we receive in return. Whichever definition we choose to embrace, the power ultimately lies in us. We can choose to stay cryogenically frozen in time or buckle up, hit the road and enjoy the ride of our messy, marvellous lives.

ETYMOLOGY: A SUMMARY

- 'The art of' something is to combine our intelligent study and observation with our creative thinking. Don't get dogmatic; get imaginative.
- Forgiveness is not toxic positivity or denying your experience.
- Forgiveness is not condoning bad behaviour, reconciling with someone or letting them off the hook. It's letting you off the hook.
- *Forgive* comes from the old English *forgiefan, which means* to give, give up or receive completely.
- Biblical times connected forgiveness to the idea of sin.
- Three Greek verbs entailed a few key elements of

forgiveness in the Bible; 'aphiemi' erasing a debt as though it never existed, 'apoluw' letting go, releasing and 'kharizomai' 'compassion and mercy.

- The Stoics believed there was no such thing as forgiveness, only forgivingness – a way of being. This centred around calmly holding on to your values and virtue, no matter what anyone else does.
- Modern definitions of forgiveness invite us to stop our negative feelings towards others and cease our punishing.

WRITING THERAPY

Writing therapy is a way of reflecting on our thoughts and feelings. It promotes self-healing and personal growth. There are many ways to do it, including journalling and expressive or creative writing. The use of writing can be a stand-alone treatment or be integrated into other therapeutic approaches.

EXERCISE

Contemplate the etymology of forgiveness. How have different ways of understanding forgiveness impacted you? Is there one definition or perspective that resonated or stood out for you? Is there one that you had an aversion to? Journal your thoughts and insights to get a sense of how this may connect to your own journey of forgiveness.

GIVING

Whether you are the transgressor or the victim, if you're interested in forgiveness, you are probably going to have to give something. In many cases, it's something you don't necessarily want to bestow. If you have caused the pain, it might mean giving an apology to acknowledge the harm caused, and space for the receiver to decide if they're ready to receive what you're offering them. This requires a generosity of spirit and a degree of courage that we may not have at the time. And it can feel unfathomable in some cases, for both the giver and receiver.

One of my favourite books is the *Bhagavad Gita*. I'm a wee bit obsessed with the wisdom it provides. A primary Hindu and yogic text, it's part of an incredible literary masterpiece, the *Mahabharata*, which was compiled by Vyasa between the 2nd and 4th centuries BCE. From

Gandhi to Einstein, it has been an inspiration for many artists, thinkers, philosophers, politicians, scientists and leaders throughout history. The Gita, as it's commonly referred to, is a conversation between Krishna, or God, and a warrior, Arjuna, who represents us mortals.

The Gita, like so many philosophical texts, explores the idea of opposites. When we look at how the universe works, for example, the law of opposites in physics, we also see this theme. Giving and receiving, inhaling and exhaling, sun and moon, yin and yang, day and night, magnets with positive and negative force, time and frequency. We need both sides of the coin. In the same relational spirit, where there is giving, there is receiving, and both parties will be affected by the action of the other.

When someone gives an apology, acknowledges a misdemeanour and takes responsibility for their part, it can free not only the receiver but the giver as well. But we can't assume everyone involved is ready. We all move at our own pace; you can't force forgiveness.

THE POWER OF AN APOLOGY

It has been said that apologies are the super glue of life. They can't undo the wrong that has been done, but they're a great first step in making it right. They can't erase mistakes, but they go a long way in repairing relationships. They show that we care about someone, respect them, regret our actions and want to do better in the future.

A 2021 Japanese study at Kobe Gakuin University, and Kobe College, Japan found that an apology is one of the most influential predictors of interpersonal forgiveness, mightier than any demographic, personality or relationship characteristic. According to researchers at the Centre for Neuroscience at the University of Bonn, Germany, when an apology was given, the empathy part of the brain of those receiving it showed increased activation. And this empathy can elicit forgiveness. In her book *The Power of Apology*, Beverly Engel explains that an apology can make the wrongdoer seem less of a threat and shows they care about the other person's feelings and are taking responsibility for their actions. She says it allows those wronged to feel respected, helps them move past anger, and creates empathy, which can elicit forgiveness.

For the giver, an apology can help eliminate feelings of remorse and shame, which can have detrimental effects on our well-being. Some people may worry that they stand to lose more by apologising, but a 2014 study by

Joost M. Leunissen and colleagues revealed this isn't the case. It suggested apologies are an important instrument for reconciliation after a transgression, and most people overestimate the negative consequences of apologising and underestimate the benefits. Taking responsibility and saying sorry can humble us, teach us valuable lessons about what not to do, and help us remain connected to our community.

However, whether an apology results in conflict resolution or not depends on the perception of the apology as trustworthy and sincere by the injured party. A 2001 cross-cultural study by professors Seiji Takaku, Bernard Weiner and Ken-Ichi Ohbuchi, from universities in Japan and the USA found that though cultural differences may affect the process, conflict is more likely to be resolved when a wrongdoer accepts personal responsibility and offers a genuine apology. Apologies for the sake of apologising, or with an agenda, generally don't work. Nor do justifications or getting defensive. An earlier meaning of 'apology' was derived from the Greek – *apologia* – which means justification, explanation, excuse or defence. For example, ancient Greek philosopher Plato's dialogue *Apologia* described Socrates' death and explained why Socrates didn't flee Athens when he was threatened with execution.

Only our more modern understanding of the word, which encompasses genuine, sincere accountability from the heart, with no excuses, is likely to bring resolution.

Though you receive a lot in the process, the spirit of giving an apology is not about what you are getting back. The key is being genuine, with no expectations of anything in return. Equally, it's important to give people the freedom, time and space to receive it in whatever way they are ready to.

ONE CONSCIOUS BREATH

I have been short-tempered and impatient in the last few weeks. While on deadline for this book, G has been home sick for over a week. It's been a long winter of working while the cost-of-living makes it impossible to play financial catch-up after those lockdown years. And the flu and bugs this season have kept us in PTSD-inducing mini-lockdown conditions. We've been in a pressure cooker of our tiny apartment, G coughing and spluttering, with a raging fever, me raging on the inside, neither of us getting any sleep, trying not to lose it with each other. I'm trying to keep him off screens all day while I am manically glued to one. Every request for food and iPad gaming time, every cough that wakes me up in the night feels like an electric shock that produces internal fires.

I've been reflecting on the anger inside me, what I'm still holding on to, and what I can't let go of. I'm still carrying a lot of sadness about so many things, and they bubble to the surface in moments like these. Having to do it all myself, not signing up for this life, and feeling like life is eternally one step forward and two steps back. When the heat is on and I'm trying to do it all as a single parent, my rumination is rampant, and my wires are frayed and they start to get frozen in unhelpful ways. I know there's not much I can do about the current situation I'm in or how it feels. But what I do know is that none of this is G's fault. And my anger towards him is misdirected.

When I get out of the shower and into my jammies, I take one big, conscious breath and tell him I'm sorry for how grouchy I've been, that it's not his fault he's sick this week while I have a lot on my plate. I'm genuinely sorry and I hope I haven't made him feel bad.

He tells me, yes, I did make him feel bad. But it's okay because he knows I'm just working hard. He just wishes I'd finish this stupid book. He gives me a big hug and then I see the cunning grin. He asks if he can have some gaming time because I've been so mean. I tell him, no, it's way too late.

He pretends to sulk and goes back to reading his book, and I sit my ass back down at the computer ready for my final stretch of the night.

The compassion and humanity of this moment feel like a huge, relieving exhale. And I know there will be more exhales. Countless parenting fails followed by 'I'm sorry'. But these little apologies every day can go a long way to building trust and love in our lives. And then there are the bigger ones that can lead us to resolution, closure or reconciliation.

The science varies on how many breaths it takes to bring us back into a state of mindfulness, from the fight-or-flight sympathetic state into the parasympathetic rest-and-digest state. But thought leader Chade-Meng Tan suggests one deep, sigh-like breath can help re-wire you in the moment, so give it a try.

THE POWER OF AN APOLOGY IN DIVORCE

Family lawyer Sarah Swan pointed out earlier that a significant challenge in family law and divorce cases when it comes to forgiveness: the underlying issue that needs forgiveness isn't the one being addressed in court. This means that even after going through a lengthy, costly and exhausting legal process, individuals may still feel a lack of justice. This is because the real source of their anger, something that the courts cannot resolve, remains unforgiven. They become trapped in this state of unforgiveness and can't move on with their lives.

She also highlights how an apology and accountability in family law cases can often quickly resolve what might otherwise become a lengthy court process. She shared a recent example where, on the very day of court, one partner wrote a letter apologising and taking responsibility for their role in causing a rupture within the family. This act of owning their part led to a final settlement that same day, avoiding the need for court proceedings. According to Swan, the simple act of apologising and acknowledging the hurt done can transform a potentially acrimonious proceeding into a more civil and functional process.

A NATIONAL APOLOGY

In 2008, the prime minister of Australia, Kevin Rudd, made a long-overdue apology to Indigenous Australians for the forced removals of their children to government agencies (a dark period of Australia's history known as the Stolen Generation). This was seen by some as progress. Tom Calma, who was the Aboriginal and Torres Strait

Islander social justice commissioner at the time, stated it laid the foundations for healing to take place. Others felt it avoided the real apology that was needed. Professor Alice MacLachlan said it avoided 'the broader question of apologizing for a much longer history of genocidal appropriation and displacement'.

We have seen reconciliation evolving in recent years. Reconciliation Australia is currently the leading body for reconciliation and they speak to the idea that it has five dimensions, all of which are interconnected. One of them – historical acceptance – is linked directly to the idea of accountability. It states:

> All Australians understand and accept the wrongs of the past and their impact on Aboriginal and Torres Strait Islander peoples. Australia makes amends for past policies and practices [and] ensures these wrongs are never repeated.
>
> **Goal:** There is widespread acceptance of our nation's history and agreement that the wrongs of the past will never be repeated – there is truth, justice, healing and historical acceptance.

Without the acknowledgement of historical facts and committing to not repeating the harm we have caused others in the past, how can we expect Indigenous peoples to trust us and feel safe to move forward? Accepting the truth of what happened and taking responsibility for it is fundamental.

TRUTH-TELLING, LISTENING, ACKNOWLEDGING

Reconciliation is going to be a long and complicated journey for us in Australia, but we are on the road to progress and it will ultimately be a rewarding path for all of us. Carla Rogers, an engagement specialist, program designer and Ally, co-founded Evolve with Aboriginal Elder Aunty Munya Andrews. The organisation runs programs that teach Indigenous cultural awareness training and Ally accreditation, with the intention of creating a kinder, more inclusive Australia. They won the 2024 Telstra Business Awards and their programs are recommended by the Australian Human Rights Commission. I have been privileged to do some webinar training with them and asked if they would be willing to talk to me about their perspectives on reconciliation and forgiveness, which they bigheartedly agreed to. We spoke about many things, some being the importance of truth-telling, listening and acknowledging as an ally. Carla said: 'You know, from just over 3 per cent of the population, this incredible gift of the oldest living continuous culture, the wisdom that's embedded in that and there's this open hand being extended to us. There needs to be truth-telling, and then we need to listen and acknowledge ... a big part of forgiveness is learning, education, hearing about the impact, listening to people's stories with an open heart. That's what you must do as an Ally, listen and acknowledge ...'

ACCOUNTABILITY IN MARRIAGE BETRAYAL

For one of my closest girlfriends, it was just an ordinary day at home with her busy toddler and four-month-old. She was one of my only mates doing proper grown-up stuff like marriage and kids. I was still doing pre-paid phone cards and fighting with flatmates. She told me this uneasy feeling had been nibbling away at her lice-like for some time, but after dragging her husband to therapy, the psychologist assured her she was just being paranoid.

Maybe it was the lack of sleep or the Molotov hormone cocktail those newborn babies serve their mums in the early days. But like an itch she couldn't scratch, her intuition kept circling her back to the mental knits that kept niggling at her. As fate would have it, there was a mindless midday chat show with an expert guest showing viewers how to catch a cheat no matter how carefully they covered their digital tracks. She jumped on the computer, and after a little history search, discovered an email account she didn't know about. Then she tried to guess the password, to no avail. She calmly called him and left a message to call back and tell her what it was. Enough time passed for her to make a hand-shaking cup of tea and stop her toddler from painting the dog. He called back, explaining it was just a burner account he used to sign up for things that he didn't want spam for, and read the combination of letters, numbers and symbols that would change her life. She opened it and found nothing but a bunch of junk emails.

But she had been educated by daytime TV, so she followed the expert's instructions and dragged the cursor down to the 'Deleted Items' folder, and there it was: a two-year affair with a co-worker. Never had she wanted to be proven wrong as he did at that moment. Her mouth was dry, her mind started to race, and she stayed like this for some time.

And so, on an average day, one of the funniest and

most family-focused people I knew began her journey of forgiveness. I remember our countless conversations at that time. I tried to be a place for her to offload whenever she needed. I don't know how helpful I was, being so young and immature and not fully comprehending the leviathan task of saving your family. She had no idea how she would ever get to the point of forgiving him, but she was determined to give it her best shot. Her parents had a strong and supportive relationship and she wanted to provide her kids with the same stability and close-knit family she had experienced growing up.

Once she agreed to save her marriage, the initial phase was long and painful. For at least six months after being caught, he kept lying about the whole situation, determined to cover his tracks. It took a lot of therapy, and hearing from friends and family, to finally come clean. He gave her the truth, or as she says, as much of it as he was willing to give.

This truth-telling part was a foundational part of the healing process for her. She needed to know what had actually happened, where the ground beneath her feet was after it had been ripped out from under her. The next step was accountability. She said to him: 'I'm not telling anyone. This is your behaviour, so you can call everyone.'

He had to face the consequences of his actions by owning up to all the people he loved and respected. In the process, he lost one of his best friends, who said: 'I can't be friends with you. You're not the kind of person I want to be around.' He also told him that what he had done to his family was criminal.

That was the beginning of their reconciliation. It was still a long, hard road to recovery after that, but telling the truth and being accountable were key to surviving the betrayal.

SEEKING FORGIVENESS

I met Rabbi Ninio many years ago when I did some classes with her. I had been studying kabbalah for some time and wanted to more deeply explore the spiritual aspects of Judaism. I recently chatted to her on a busy Monday to talk about forgiveness and the wisdom Judaism has to share.

Rabbi Ninio spoke about Yom Kippur, an important date on the Jewish calendar, known as the Day of Atonement. This day repairs your relationship with God, *but* it does not repair your relationship with people. For that, you must go to the person and seek forgiveness. 'You have to do the work,' she says. 'It's not enough to say a few prayers and say you're sorry. That's not forgiveness. That's not repentance.

That's not change. You need to be changed as a result.'

She explains that though the tradition emphasises the importance of seeking forgiveness for wrongs committed, it comes with a caveat; if the person is not able to forgive, for whatever reason, after you have made three genuine, heartfelt attempts to seek forgiveness, then that's enough. There is a compassionate understanding that it may be traumatising for a person to feel they have to forgive something when they can't.

On reflecting post chat with Rabbi Ninio, I'm struck by how powerful this idea is. We must repair our relationships, seek forgiveness, change and do the work ourselves. But we cannot assume the other party is ready. Forgiveness is something we need to proactively work at, but it is not something we can force.

THE IMPORTANCE OF AN APOLOGY

The Quran holds forgiveness as a central theme and Islam embraces the value of an apology. I spoke to Mai Elbasandili, a positive psychology coach and Youth College Manager of the Islamic Sciences and Research Academy of Australia at Charles Sturt University. Mai tells me:

In Islam, forgiveness is encouraged, but it is also essential to recognize the importance of setting boundaries and maintaining accountability. When someone wrongs another person, they are required to seek forgiveness from both God (Allah) and the individual they have harmed. God forgives all sins committed against Him when a person sincerely repents. However, if someone has wronged another human being, they must first address the issue with the person they hurt before seeking forgiveness from Allah. Islam teaches that humans should be forgiving, and if someone genuinely asks for forgiveness, the wronged person should be willing to forgive them.

Apologising does not mean that consequences vanish. If I mistakenly raise my voice at my children, I should apologise and seek their forgiveness; however, they need to understand the importance of correcting their behaviour. Similarly, when a child breaks a rule, a parent can forgive them while still enforcing appropriate consequences. This balance fosters compassion, fairness and mutual respect.

MAGGIE DENT ON APOLOGIES AND ACCOUNTABILITY IN PARENTING

Parenting author and educator Maggie Dent echoes the importance of apologising when we mess up, not only to deepen our relationship with our kids but to also model the behaviour that will be helpful for them as adults. She also talks about accountability and how fundamental it is for kids to understand it and practise it, especially boys, who need to move around more and have physical fun. This can contribute to poor choices, which sometimes cause harm. As parents, we need to help them understand that what they've done isn't okay and that they've caused some damage. Then we need to empower them to make choices about how to make it right. And here's the kicker – we must make sure they do it. Because they will forget. Anyone with an eleven-year-old boy will know how hard it is for them to remember water bottles, jumpers, school bags, sporting equipment or anything not physically attached to them. If they can't remember everyday things, they won't remember to apologise to the teacher or friend for what they did the day before. Maggie tells me: 'Gentle reminders need to be done warmly, with connection first, in order to be effective. Positive noticing when they do the right thing and make amends is also really helpful.'

Then, she says, what is crucial is to forgive and forget. Otherwise, it's going to eat away at their self-worth, turning guilt into shame, which doesn't help anyone. As parents, we must model all this behaviour. When we mess up, lose our shit or behave in ways we are not proud of, we have to own it, apologise to our kids with transparency and humility, and make amends in the same way we would expect them to.

Whether you are on the giving or receiving end, an apology, the truth, accountability and repentance can be the very things that make forgiveness possible. The 'giving' in forgiving may help you forge your way forward, and a slow exhale may bring you into a mindful state so you can do it.

GIVING: A SUMMARY

- Forgiveness often requires giving something.
- The act of giving, such as an apology, can positively impact both the giver and receiver.
- Apologies, though they cannot undo wrongs, are essential for repairing relationships.
- Apologies must be genuine, without justification or defence, and acknowledge the wrongdoing.

- The 2008 National Apology to Indigenous Australians is seen as progress towards healing but remains controversial for not addressing the broader historical wrongs. Historical acceptance and accountability are key to progress in reconciliation.
- Reconciliation in Australia involves truth-telling and the acknowledgement of past wrongs. Listening to and learning from those wronged is essential.
- In cases of infidelity, telling the truth and being accountable are often crucial to the healing process.
- Yom Kippur is an important Jewish Day of Atonement that repairs your relationship with God but not with people. For that, you must seek forgiveness directly from the person harmed.
- Though you must seek forgiveness, you cannot assume the other party is ready. Forgiveness can't be forced.
- In Islam, you cannot seek forgiveness from God if you haven't made amends with the person you harmed.
- Maggie Dent stresses the importance of parents modelling accountability. They can do this by apologising for their own mistakes and teaching kids to take responsibility, make amends and move forward without letting guilt turn into shame.

APOLOGY FRAMEWORK

The late psychiatrist Aaron Lazare was the chancellor and dean of the University of Massachusetts Medical School and an apology expert. In his book *On Apology*, he unpacks the complexities and importance of apologising and distils how to do it into four simple steps. If you're contemplating apologising but are unsure how to do it, here is a framework. Be creative with how you use it. Get clear on your intention, have no expectation of results, and use real, justification-free language.

EXERCISE

Think of a situation that requires an apology. It may be something you have done, or perhaps something you didn't do. It could be from the present or the past. Put the framework into practice.

1. Acknowledgement of the offence - take responsibility for your behaviour, avoiding language that is vague or minimises their experience.
2. Explain what happened - this is your perspective, but without justification or excuses.
3. Express remorse - if you genuinely feel guilt, let them know.
4. Offer to make amends - commit to action that can repair or not repeat that behaviour in the future.

GIVING COMPLETELY

There may come a time when we feel we've really messed up, when no amount of apologising or accountability will cut it and there is too much pain to turn things around, when things feel impossible to resolve or confusion reigns over clarity. In those moments, when you're on your knees and crying, 'I don't know what to do, tell me what to do', offer it up. Many religions, including Christianity, Hinduism and Islam suggest the ultimate act of giving is to offer everything up to something greater than yourself. Call it what you will – the universe, or God – and take all your guilt, anger, bitterness, shame or suffering and give it to a higher power.

Mai tells me that when it's too heavy to forgive, give it to God to carry: 'I know it's really hard, when you have a deep wound in your heart. When someone really, really hurts you. In Islam, it's okay not to forgive them. God will take care of it. So, you can let it go. Let it go out of your heart. Give it to something more powerful – to God. So you don't carry it anymore. Allah does.'

The Gita has a very similar teaching, considered to be one of the most important in Hinduism. In chapter nine, Krishna reveals 'the great secret' to Arjuna. Eknath Easwaran's translation is this: 'Whatever I am offered in devotion with a pure heart – a leaf, a flower, fruit or water – I accept with joy. Whatever you do, make it an offering to me – the food you eat, the sacrifices you make, the help you give, even your suffering.'

The big secret of this vast piece of epic wisdom is to surrender it all, even your suffering. The ultimate act of giving becomes your ticket to peace. This is the essence of bhakti yoga, which is connected to the idea of devotion, offering everything up to something greater than yourself. Bhakti yogis take this wisdom and live their life by it. Every action is an offering, with no attachment – just love and devotion.

BHAKTI – DEVOTION

My favourite bhakti yogi is Keith Kempis. Keith is a performer, music and yoga teacher. The owner of Bija Yoga studio in Penrith, Sydney, Keith has been teaching for over twenty years and we met almost that long ago through our dedication to Jivamukti yoga. We share many of the same teachers as well as our warped sense of humour and a love for all things art and yoga. As a bhakti yogi, he talks about how devotion helps us remember our sameness, not our difference:

> Bhakti means to be devoted … to someone or something higher than the small self which is bound by ego and is ultimately self-serving. It requires us to go far beyond rational thought.
>
> The rational mind can say 'I can forgive BUT I CANNOT forget', but the heart, although hurt and in desperate need of healing, can say 'I HAVE to forgive in order to forget'.

Bhakti asks us to see divinity in others, to see their highest potential and to believe in this potential. A good way to start our bhakti practice is to replace 'I can forgive but I cannot forget' with 'may all beings – including and especially those who I feel have wronged me – be happy and free and may everything I think, say and do contribute in some way to that freedom. It is only in this way that I can reach my highest potential.' If we say this repeatedly (even if it's silent), we'll start to see those who have hurt us are hurt too and therefore in need of forgiveness.

SO BE IT

I am not a tattoo person, but if I were ever to get one, this would probably be it – '*svaha*.' It is a Sanskrit word used at the end of a mantra that means 'so be it.' It is also connected to fire rituals, where you are literally offering it all up to the sacred fire. I use it every day, just to let things fall away and burn. But for the big things, it is the perfect word for those moments when I feel like I am stuck, burning, heartbroken, furious or just can't let it go. I've done all I can. I don't know what else to do. Instead of burning shit down (which I would like to do), I give it to the sacred fire. It's not a flippant 'mate, drop it, let it go.' It's an invitation for something greater than myself to step in and help. Because, quite honestly, it all feels beyond me sometimes. And all I can do is say, 'svaha.'

SWIM IN THE WORLD WITH ONE HAND, HOLD GOD'S WITH THE OTHER

It's a winter evening in Sydney, and I'm wearing a presentable cream sweater on top (and pyjama pants on the bottom), waiting for my video call with teacher Seema Johari. Keith has suggested I connect with Seema to understand what Hinduism says about forgiveness. Keith speaks about her with such love, humility and respect, and I have always wanted to meet her. One day, when G is a bit older, I hope to go to her centre in India, study with her and bathe in her presence. But for now, I make the most of grabbing a brief window in time with her while G is at basketball, and I have a parent dropping him home later, so I can be totally present.

Seema Johari Agarwal is the daughter of Master Harish Johari, considered one of the world's foremost teachers of sacred Hindu texts. He was also a visual artist of international renown. It was through his art that he often communicated his teachings as he felt it was a powerful way to reach a wider community viscerally. Seema teaches throughout Europe, North America, Australia and at the Johari family compound in India.

Cradling my cup of 'relaxing tea', I'm not at all relaxed, nervous and excited to be in her presence. When Seema appears on the iPhone screen, sitting in her bedroom in Haridwar, North India, her beaming round face is bright, like the colours on her loose, cotton top. She's just finished her usual vegetarian lunch: dahl, rice, vegetables, roti and salad pickles, prepared and cooked based on Ayurvedic principles. For someone with such extraordinary ancestry and knowledge, she embodies what all the most evolved and truly 'spiritual' people I have met possess: humility, humour and joy. She carries no hierarchy or arrogance and immediately puts me at ease in her disarming, charming way. She has me laughing straightaway and meanders between engaging stories and mic-dropping moments of profound wisdom.

Growing up, surrounded by her father's great work and teachings, she initially didn't realise the significance of it. She married young and went off to Delhi to start her family life. It wasn't until her father's passing in 1999, when her mother asked her to move back to the family house, that she started to fully comprehend his legacy. And so she decided to honour him by realising his dream of creating a home for his students. She started running retreats at the family compound, and her business, Spiritual Vacations, still operates in this sacred space.

I was brought up by my beloved grandpa, who was Catholic, and an atheist mum who liked to use bits of it when it suited her. Whenever I was pushing boundaries, doing something I wasn't meant to do, standing too close to the flames and getting burnt, my mum was suddenly Catholic too.

'Well, that's your guardian angel teaching you a lesson,' she'd caution.

That wasn't the point of guardian angels, but it did mean I grew up terrified that some higher being saw everything I did and was prepared to punish me accordingly. Until I practised yoga, I understood karma in a similar way, like some judgy karma angel was eternally watching me. Or I'd been born with bad luck, which I could conveniently call karma.

If anyone hadn't heard of karma before Taylor Swift came along, she's made sure we're acquainted with it now. Look, I love Tay Tay, went to the show, swapped the bracelets, but she, like most of us, misunderstands what karma is and how it works. Even G, my eleven-year-old, will mutter that karma will take care of it when something goes wrong. It's misused in the same way my mum took poetic licence with guardian angels and parents use Santa to get good behaviour in the lead-up to Christmas.

The truth of how karma works, according to ancient

teachings popularised in yoga, Hinduism and especially the Gita, is far more complex and powerful. And it puts us back in the driver's seat rather than having some imaginary external being running the show and taking care of business for us. And Seema tells me that a basic understanding of karma is crucial when working with forgiveness:

> When you don't forgive, you're creating negative karmas. And the Gita is about washing away the karmas. Krishna says, 'Don't do any karma ... not even good, not even bad. Do only what is right. Do only what you're supposed to. Do only what is your karma. But with fullness of me in your mind so that you don't create more karmas.'

Our old karmas, she tells me, all the sufferings we experience in this life, come from our past actions. And what we are doing now will determine our future karma, our suffering – either now or in the next life. The idea of being a spiritual person is to break our patterns so we don't have to keep getting the same lessons in this life and the next. The problem is that everything we do creates karma. Every action has a reaction or counteraction – breathing, eating, everything we do – which is why Seema says we must learn to become conscious in everything we do and make skilful choices.

As the Stoics said, get clear on your virtues, ethics, principles and values and live a life based on them. Let go of attachment to the results of your actions. Do your best to be a good person and expect nothing in return. You do you and let them do them. But the most important thing is to completely surrender and make all your actions an offering. Seema says:

> Krishna says ... Surrender towards me. Do something for the sake of just goodness. For ethics, for morality, for the sake of doing something with *no* selfish motive. And have me in your heart. I always say, keep holding God's hand with one hand, and swim in the world. Then you'll never be lost. You'll never drown.

When in doubt, give completely. Let go and let God, which is not throwing your hands up in despair. Rather, live your ethics and be conscious in your actions, but when it all feels like it's too much ... svaha.

GIVING COMPLETELY: A SUMMARY

- Release your anger and pain and offer it up to a higher power.
- Devotion helps us see divinity in others and realise our shared humanity, enabling forgiveness.
- Svaha. So be it. Give it all to the sacred fire.
- Conscious actions reduce negative karma and aid forgiveness.
- Swim in the world with one hand and hold God's with the other. Stay connected to a higher power.

SERENITY PRAYER

Authorship of the now infamous Serenity Prayer has been disputed over the years. Perhaps it was penned by Greek philosopher Aristotle, Roman citizen Boetius, St Francis of Assisi, St Thomas Aquinas or Reinhold Niebuhr. The Serenity Prayer was popularised by the Young Women's Christian Association in the 1930s and then Alcoholics Anonymous in the 1940s. Today, it is considered a powerful invocation of acceptance, courage and wisdom.

EXERCISE

You can say this invocation quietly to yourself, anywhere, anytime. Or choose a comfortable seat, close your eyes, and offer it up sincerely as a stand-alone practice. You could also add the Sanskrit word 'svaha' at the end to emphasise you really mean it.

God, grant me the serenity to accept the things I cannot change, the courage to change the things I can, and the wisdom to know the difference.

GIVING UP

A few years ago, I went through a mediation to resolve a situation where there was some spicy conflict. I got wonderful advice from a friend at the time who was a corporate mediator herself. She told me that if I wanted resolution, which I did, I would have to give up something I really didn't want to. This piece of advice was invaluable and allowed me some time and space before the mediation to contemplate what I didn't want to give up. The conflict was creating friction on a daily basis and the trade-off for a more peaceful life was to make a conscious sacrifice.

THE UNIVERSAL DEAL – TAPAS

In yoga, one of the key themes is '*tapas*', which can be viewed as discipline and austerity or sacrifice. The universal deal is you can have whatever you want, but you have to give something up. Want to get fit? You might have to give up half an hour of sleep or scrolling on your phone. Want to write a book in your spare time? If you're also working and parenting, like me, you might have to give up time with friends, family and other aspects of your life that give you joy. Similarly, we must give up something in the process of forgiveness, especially where there is conflict, if we want to move forward.

GIVE UP HOPE FOR A BETTER PAST

When you compromise or sacrifice during forgiveness, it also means giving up your attachment to wanting things to be different. As my yoga teacher, David Life, used to say, 'What's done is done.' I was also given a brutal but powerful mantra by shaman and sound healer Gareth Mansell when I was in the depths of my post-separation baby blues: 'So what, now what?' Every time I went down a rabbit hole of despair, it was a short cut to pull me back out. It drew me quickly from the past, which I couldn't change, and into the present. It's a great check in, when you feel yourself slipping into wanting things to be different, to say to yourself yes, okay, that has happened, it wasn't great, but what are you going to do now? You must give up a version of reality you don't get to live. It reminded me of a quote attributed to Anne Lamont: 'forgiveness is giving up all hope for a better past.' I had to grieve so many things before I could even begin to move on. And the biggest one was the idea of what life with a family would look like – a future that was not to be.

GIVING UP IN LAYERS THROUGH ART

There are times when words fail us. When the suffering we endure is too much and we don't know how to give up the pain or process it in any way. When so many other ways to deal with our emotions have failed us, art can play a very powerful role in forgiveness, as it is a means to express our internal conflicts and feelings through creativity and symbolism in a physical way. It connects us to play, we can make a mess and tell stories to work through layers of forgiveness with our own personal, imaginative approach.

Nasim Nasr is an Iranian-born, Australian award-winning visual artist based in Sydney. Her artworks have been exhibited nationally and internationally since 2010 and placed in numerous public institutions in Australia, and private collections around the world. We meet at her studio and sit at a micro round table where she serves us Persian tea and treats. We are surrounded by volumes of framed images and TV screens playing videos of eyes and hands.

As a young, talented art student in Iran, Nasim created nude drawings and paintings of the feminine form, a subject she loved, but forbidden under the Islamic Republic's laws. Despite graduating with the highest score, she couldn't showcase her work, as if she did exhibit them, she would have faced the constant threat of imprisonment.

'Being a woman, an artist, with the subject matter we chose, it was a daily risk. If you are caught, you never know what will happen to you next. It's a red zone so I just faced the risk of getting caught and going to prison on a daily basis.'

Inspired by artists like Shirin Neshat and Marjane Satrapi, Nasim knew leaving Iran was her only chance to ensure her safety and use her art to amplify the voices of oppressed Iranian women. In 2009, with great effort, her family secured her a student visa to study in Australia, where she also took on raising her younger siblings. In stark contrast to Iran's restrictive laws, her visit to Maslin Beach, South Australia's first official nude beach, profoundly impacted her. The beach's rules required that she not wear anything, or she would face a fine. This was a stark contrast to the

Iran she had grown up in, where exposing any hair or part of the body as a woman could lead to severe punishment, including fines, imprisonment or worse. The contradiction was overwhelming, and it marked the beginning of her moving on from her past through her artwork.

During that pivotal visit to Maslin Beach, she created one of her most significant early works, *Liberation* (2009–2010). She took her grandmother's covering and held it in front of her, standing among the nude beachgoers, and took a series of photos. This symbolic act, a visual representation of the tension between her past and her present, became her most published work. But more importantly, it marked a turning point in her artistic career. After that, she had a new form of expression through the lens of a camera. She describes this to me as an act of forgiveness in the context of giving up. She says:

'From that moment, I didn't want to do painting and drawing anymore. The act of forgiveness was just to give up everything I knew; my country, my past, the way I made art ... forgiveness for people of oppressive countries, the way we can forgive the government and how they treat us, is just to leave it all behind.'

Her next work, *Erasure* (2009–2010), was a ten-minute

video. In it, you can see a hand, her sister's, writing words in chalk on a chalkboard. These words are memories, and as her sister writes snippets of her past, Nasim erases them behind her. They are written in two languages, Farsi, their native language, and English, the new language of their new life. But as Nasim tries to wipe the chalk off, it doesn't totally disappear from the board. There are smudged remnants of the words left behind.

This artwork deals with the notion of trying hard to erase your past but being unable to expunge everything. There are always traces left behind. 'It helped me to forgive what had happened at home, just by writing it,' says Nasim. 'You give up everything, you leave your home, but it's always there ... what happens to women at home, it was hurting my soul. It still does. So, the only way I could forgive my past was just to keep making the work I have made.'

Another deeply symbolic work about giving up your past is *33 Beads* (2017). It refers to the string of thirty-three praying beads religious men in Iran carry. In a photographic series of thirteen images and video, she is holding a string of these beads. In each image, her face is shrouded behind her hair, so we can't tell if she is about to break them apart or hold onto them. In the video, we see her finally breaking them, releasing the tension, as she no longer wants to have the past with her. But at the same time, she introduces the idea of needing her community, her new life, to help her do it:

> In the video, you'll see clearly, eventually, a lot of female hands come together, and they help me to break it. You know, forgiveness, sometimes it's hard to do it alone. You need a lot of hands to come together and help to break the beads, break the tradition, break the circle.

Nasim's works make me realise that giving up something to move on with your life is no easy thing. Even when you must do it for your fundamental safety, when it's life or death. Attachment is hard, as we will explore in later chapters, and sometimes, the only way to give up your past and move towards your future is to be creative with the solution. It doesn't have to happen all at once, in one big gesture. The past may not ever be totally erased, but we can give up our attachment and connection to it bit by bit.

GIVING UP: A SUMMARY

- To resolve conflict, you'll probably have to give up something significant, something you may not want to give up.
- The universal deal in yoga is centred around one of the key teachings – *tapas* (discipline/sacrifice). To gain something, you must give something up.
- Give up hope for a better past.
- Iranian-Australian artist Nasim Nasr uses her art to give up her past and build a future.
- Forgiveness and moving forward are gradual.

YOGA NIDRA

Yoga nidra is the yoga of sleep. It is a guided meditation practice taken lying on your back. A 2024 study by Aigerim Tastanova and colleagues found that there was a positive relationship between yoga nidra and creativity and cognitive flexibility. And research in 2022 by Seithikurippu R Pandi-Perumal and colleagues showed that yoga nidra was powerful in reducing stress anxiety and depression, and improving physical and mental health.

EXERCISE

There are many yoga nidra guided meditations online. I suggest getting on your favourite streaming platform and listening to different voices to see which one appeals to you.

I have a mini yoga nidra available at www.abc.net.au/listen/programs/classicflow/mini-meditation-mini-nidra/10706366.

LETTING GO

Whether you believe in Christianity, Hinduism, Islam, the ancient Greeks, family law or my grandpa, they all preach that to forgive you have to let go. Letting things go doesn't necessarily mean acceptance. It just means you don't let things stick; you drop them and move on. I know this is easier said than done. And sometimes, letting go is only possible when there is a boundary in place and we feel safe enough to do so. We let go of little things every day but letting go of the big things can be overwhelming for most people. Perhaps it's our anger and resentment, or a need to be right that makes it so hard. It may take a lot of courage, but we have the wisdom of the ancients to help us work towards letting go.

LET GO AND LET GOD

When I was suspended from high school for smoking in an out-of-bounds area, I was furious because I wasn't even smoking. I was just pretending so I could hang with the cool kids. Mum flew me to Canberra to spend the week with Grandpa because she was working and not at all happy I'd got myself into this predicament. After I got off the plane, I lamented to Grandpa that it felt unjust. My very Catholic grandpa smiled and told me it was a wonderful lesson. And then he said the thing he would continue to tell me whenever I was struggling with powerful emotions or challenging situations: 'My darling, let go and let God.'

My ADHD/anxiety brain has always had a nuclear grade capacity to ruminate. But this time, because of my beloved grandpa, I dropped it. And we ended up having an incredibly rewarding, fun week together, one of the most impactful times spent with him. He took me to the Australian War Memorial and as we walked through, I felt his deep connection to the stories as he had served in World War II and lost brothers and friends in both wars. We wandered through the National Art Gallery of Australia and I fell in love with art. I went to church every morning with him and felt my nervous system calm in the quietness and sacred ritual of it all. He bought me a rosary and a book, *Are You There God? It's Me, Margaret,* which I believe set me on the spiritual path I still find myself on to this day. I'm still an avid reader, art-lover and the rosary beads have given way to mala beads in meditation instead.

During my conversation with Seema, I talked about the concept of letting go being part of forgiveness. In response, she told me a story I wish I had heard when I was a kid. I shared it with G that night and it's become a daily mantra for us. Here's what Seema said:

> When I was a small girl, someone would upset me, and I used to come to my mother and say, 'She did this' or 'She spoke like this to me'. And my mother would say, 'Did it stick to you?'
>
> I would be more upset and say, 'I was telling you something, such a big thing that happened to me.' And she used to always simply say, 'Did it stick to you? It will only hurt you if you feel it. Don't feel it. Forget it.'
>
> We were trained like this from the beginning, you know, because we used to live in a joint family. My auntie was there, her four sons were there, we

> were there, my three sisters were there. We had always so many guests, so many people coming and going. So as a child, there could always be a clash with anybody. And so my mother would say, 'Did it stick to you?'
>
> Later, when I grew up, I really felt it. Did it stick to me? No. It will only stick to you when you want it.

If we practised this trick of not letting little things stick to us from a young age, I wonder if it would help us with the bigger ones later in life. When it feels like the superglue has taken hold and we are 'roos in headlights, unable to break the circuit, would the lifelong practice make it more achievable?

So next time someone tries to harm you with their words or actions, remember this: Did it stick to you? No, not today!

LETTING GO OF GRUDGES AS A DAILY PRACTICE

Peter Gould, a designer and entrepreneur, has been exploring Islam and the spiritual path for just over 20 years. He explains that there are a lot of beautiful stories in the Islamic tradition and a long series of messengers and prophets who came over millennia. These include great teachers like Jesus and Moses and many others who are revered in the faith.

Muhammad is considered the last of these prophets, the one who 'brought the final message for the benefit of all'. Many records exist of how he interacted with people, serving as an example for others to learn from. This reminds me of Christianity, where there are similar stories of Jesus embodying his teachings around compassion and non-judgement. Encounters with the prophets in Islam are well documented and Peter shares one about Muhammad, who at the time was in Medina, modern-day Saudi Arabia, where he lived.

On this day, Muhammad was sharing his wisdom with a group of companions, when he mentioned that someone would soon join them. This person, he said, was among the people of paradise, which meant he was very successful in how he lived and worked. Of course, everyone was curious about him and what made him so special. When he arrived, one of the cohort, Abdullah, followed him for three days and nights, watching his actions, but he didn't notice anything exceptional. The man prayed and fasted just like everyone else, so what was his secret?

Abdullah approached the man and asked: 'What makes you deserve that really amazing status?'

The man replied: 'I don't do anything special, except before I sleep every night, I make sure I don't hold any grudge against any person so I can sleep with a clean heart.'

Because of that, he's given paradise, an eternal, exquisite garden.

That garden brings us a state of inner peace. So one of the rewards of forgiving is to preserve the serenity of your own mind. When we give up our grudges against others, even if it's just in our minds, the result is a personal paradise.

Similarly, Aristotle said: 'The great-spirited man is not a grudge-bearer either; for it is not a great-spirited person's part to keep a record of other people's deeds, especially not their misdeeds; but rather to overlook them.'

LETTING GO OF ATTACHMENTS

Yoga is a state of peace and wholeness. Nothing is missing, and you are missing nothing. So, by its very nature, wholeness and hatred can't co-exist. When we practice yoga, we start to unravel the sticky nature of resentment. Yogic tools are there to assist us in becoming whole again, remembering who we are beyond the external world and all the things that trigger us. The more we connect to that deeper, complete part of ourselves, connected to something greater than our individual story, the more we can take a bird's-eye view and observe our part in the game of life. Yes, there will be suffering, but there will also be joy and love. As Seema said earlier, when speaking of karma, the trick is in letting go of attachment to results. And as yoga and Buddhism tell us, it's also about letting go of our attachment to big emotions. As Buddha said, 'The root of suffering is attachment.'

Siddartha Gautama was born in South Asia, which we now know as Nepal, in the 5th or 6th century BCE. Part of an aristocratic family, he had everything he would ever need in life but renounced it all to go on a journey in search of the truth. He decided to sit in meditation under a Bodhi tree until he discovered why people suffered and how he could put an end to it. After forty-nine days he reached enlightenment and spent the rest of his life teaching what we now call Buddhism. In Buddhism, it is said that suffering is caused by attachment. Therefore, what we are letting go of in forgiveness are our attachments, especially to pesky things called the 'kleshas'.

GETTING TRIGGERED

You're chatting to a new friend at a party. It's all going well and suddenly … there it is. You don't know what you said, but they pull away from you. A wall comes up. Conversely, you could be at work, grabbing a coffee with a co-worker, and they say something. You feel it in your body like a bullet and your whole being wants to withdraw. In Buddhism, this is called 'shenpa', our human tendency to get triggered by others. It hooks us, creates strong emotions, and causes us to shut down.

These strong emotions, known as the 'kleshas', include ignorance, anger, craving, pride and jealousy. Shenpa is related to our attachment to things. We are attached to our kleshas, which is what causes our suffering. As Pema Chödrön, a Western Tibetan nun and author, says in an article for *Lion's Roar*: 'When we realize that we like our kleshas, we begin to understand why they have such power over us. Hatred, for example, can make us feel strong and in charge. Rage makes us feel even more powerful and invulnerable.'

But when those big feelings arise and we are triggered, we have two options: to pause, feel and respond consciously; or, to react directly to the trigger, which is what we usually do. And that generally doesn't go so well.

It's not just Buddhism that suggests attachment to the kleshas is the core of our suffering. The great yogi and sage Patanjali also refers to them in the second chapter of the *Yoga Sutras*, one of the primary yogic texts compiled between the 5th and 4th century BCE.

ATTACHMENT AND AVERSION

In the *Yoga Sutras*, the kleshas are described as afflictions of the mind, obstacles to enlightenment or peace. Most of us don't spend any time feeling connected to something greater. But without that connection with universal consciousness, the universe, God, we become attached to the ego. We focus on the body, mind and personality rather than anchoring to the deeper part of ourselves. So, we protect the ego (especially from pain or distress), as though it's a matter of life or death – because it is. If we believe we are just the ego, and the ego dies, then we die too – the party is over. So we end up bouncing between people, places and things we like (*raga),* and moving away from those we have an aversion to (*dvesha)*. Ultimately, we spend our life ping-ponging between these opposing states: attachment and aversion, like and dislike, love and hate.

THE HARDENING EFFECT

Just like the 'stuckness' and rumination we spoke about earlier, constantly moving between attachment and aversion has a reinforcing quality. It becomes ingrained, we expect it, and every time we circle back to the feeling of deep clinging or hostility, it strengthens and hardens around us. We need to start noticing how often we get caught up in those thoughts and feelings and catch ourselves in the process. Every time we feel strong emotions thanks to our attachment to the kleshas, and lapse into old behaviour patterns to avoid pain, we reinforce the tendency. We are addicted to our kleshas, and so both Buddhism and yoga tell us to let go of our attachments to stop the suffering. It's okay to feel anger, but then we must drop it and move on. Otherwise, it will harden and we can end up like 'roos in headlights.

When we pause and sit with the darker parts of ourselves, allowing emotional responses to rise (as they inevitably will), we can see where we are still stuck. The pause allows an opportunity for self-knowledge. We receive insight as to what needs to be resolved and healed. Pain is part of the human condition, and instead of avoiding it, a moment of stillness allows us to face it head-on. Pema

Chödrön refers to this as 'leaning into the needle' instead of continually backing away, reacting and reinforcing our attachment.

LOVE-HATE PING-PONG

As humans, we often get stuck in the never-ending ping-pong game between love and hate. Attachment starts super sneakily, with a little spark of desire. We want something, which activates the brain's reward system. As we move towards it, we feel a sense of pleasure, and we are served a good dopamine-serotonin-happy-chemical cocktail. The more we get, the more we want, and desire turns into craving. This is where addiction and obsession can stem from. We mistake these fleeting moments of joy for true happiness. We forget that the spark comes from within, that deeper part of ourselves. When we have undue attachment to something, it can only end in pain.

Just as we tend to move towards the people we like, we move away from those we dislike. It's normal to not get along with everyone. We are all very different snowflakes. But aversion takes us further away from a state of peace, and we are the ones who pay the price, not the people we hate. We see this time and time again, where love ends and hatred begins. Two people who once couldn't keep their hands off one another now cannot stand being in the same room.

IMPERMANENCE

One of our greatest lessons from undue attachment is the reality that all things end. Everything is in an eternal state of change. Things begin, sustain for a period of time – none of us know how long – and then they end. If we lie to ourselves about what this life is, we will suffer. Love changes and ends, and the pain of this reality often morphs into hate. Unless you are a vampire or a white walker, nothing and no one you love is immortal. The more comfortable we become with impermanence, the easier it is to love without expectation. The love that sits underneath our connections with others never disappears. It comes from inside of us and is eternal.

The more we let go of our attachment to holding on to things and not wanting them to change or end, the easier it will be to forgive when the seasons of life and the people we love transform – as they always do.

HATRED STEALS YOUR ENERGY

Where the goal of spiritual practices is to create more unity, aversion is the great separator. It creates division and requires a lot of energy. Hatred is like a whirlpool that bleeds us dry and steals our attention. Think of how often our minds have circled back to that person who hurt us. All that time and energy we wasted on someone who doesn't know or care. And yet we let them hijack our consciousness. Think of where else in your life all that energy could go!

You're going to love some people more than others. That's just the reality of being human. Get interested in how you value some people and things more than others, how you attach to the ones you like and try to get as much distance as possible from the ones you don't. When aversion turns to hatred, that's when the real work begins. Getting curious about what is sitting underneath deep aversion will foster powerful self-knowledge. My greatest learning has come from people I have found it almost impossible to forgive or build a bridge with. I'm so grateful I've had those experiences to understand who I really am and soften those rigid parts of myself. They have fostered empathy both for my own imperfections and others'. Don't be afraid of hatred, but don't let it steal your energy and attention. Do what you can to understand where it comes from and act from that place.

JUDGEMENT

When we judge, we are creating distance. Often that is because we feel unsafe in some way. Sometimes there are good reasons for that feeling; it's our intuition sensing danger. In that case, a boundary may need to be set to keep us safe. Sometimes there's no threat, just repulsion showing us where some work is still to be done inside ourselves. It may be our conditioning creating an unnecessary division. Judgement is the beginning of hatred, so observe how it plays out in you. Instead of creating distance, it may be that all we need to get grounded and foster connectivity rather than separation. As Pema Chödrön says:

> We have a choice. We can spend our whole life suffering because we can't relax with how things really are, or we can relax and embrace the open-endedness of the human situation, which is fresh, unfixated, unbiased. So the challenge is to notice the emotional tug of shenpa when it arises.

BIAS

Amber Cardozo is a senior policy maker. Her career is defined by a commitment to fostering equality, inclusivity and harmony in Australian communities. Currently, she is dedicated to combating religious intolerance and promoting social cohesion through strategies that address religious discrimination and foster inclusion across communities. As she is passionate about building a more tolerant, inclusive world, and has experience applying these strategies in real world settings, she is well placed to speak to what really gets in the way of forgiveness.

Amber believes it's essential to address internal bias. Forgiveness cannot be fully understood and practised without recognising the biases that influence our actions and decisions. These biases are often deeply ingrained and reinforced by our personal experiences. Whenever we come in with bias, we're quite blocked and resistant to change, so we need to address that before we embrace forgiveness.

She says: 'Internal bias comes from generations, it comes from cultures, and our own culture as well. We need to face the internal bias sits within all of us. Now, for example, I am really confronted by this in my work. I'm working in the space of religious intolerance. So, it's making me really have to question my own bias, look at my own belief systems, and challenge them. Which is not a simple task to do. I think shame gets woven in there, and a little bit of bigotry, and all sorts of different things. But we have to face that part of ourselves if we want to move towards forgiveness.'

Self-examination and untangling emotions in this way is not easy, but it's the only way forward if we want to move past our limited views of the world towards a more tolerant and accepting planet.

MIND YOUR OWN BUSINESS

Rather than judging, which pulls us outside ourselves to things beyond our control, we can direct our awareness inside, to the stuff we can control. The Bible shares this perspective: "How can you say to your brother, 'Let me take the speck out of your eye,' when all the time there is a plank in your own eye? You hypocrite, first take the plank out of your own eye, and then you will see clearly to remove the speck from your brother's eye. (*Bible – New International Version*, Matthew 7:3–5)."

LETTING GO: A SUMMARY

- Let go and let God.

- When something upsets you, ask yourself: 'Did it stick?' It will only stick if you let it.
- Forgive your grudges every night – that's the way to your internal paradise.
- Letting go of our attachment to big emotions is key to ending our suffering.
- Strong emotional reactions, called *shenpa* in Buddhism, can hook us.
- Attachment and aversion trap us in a cycle of suffering, but by practising detachment from both pleasure and pain, we achieve freedom.
- Hostile and attached feelings can reinforce themselves and have a hardening effect.
- Sitting with uncomfortable emotions allows insight and healing. Pause, feel, let go.
- Everything changes and ends.
- Aversion drains our energy.
- Judging others creates division.
- We need to confront our biases.
- We cannot control others, only our reactions.

LET GO MEDITATION

My yoga teachers, Jivamukti Yoga founders, Sharon Gannon and David Life, taught me this simple mantra meditation. I have practised many forms of meditation over the years, but this one I have circled back to throughout my life due to its simplicity and accessibility.

EXERCISE

Choose a comfortable seat and close your eyes. Bring awareness into your physical body and notice how your body, mind and breath feel. Commit to stillness for this brief time. Breathe in and out through the nostrils. Don't modify it. Allow it to move freely and naturally. As you inhale, think of the word LET, and as you exhale, think of the word GO. Inhaling LET, exhaling GO. The mind will wander. That's okay. That's the job of the mind. Our role is to notice where the mind has wandered and come back to the breath. Inhaling LET and exhaling GO.

You could set a timer for five minutes. When you're finished, bring your awareness back to the breath, allowing the mantra to drop away. Notice the breath, the physical body and the mind. Take a deep, slow inhalation and exhale to let the breath go.

You can find me guiding a five-minute recorded version of this meditation with some classical music underneath at www.abc.net.au/listen/programs/classicflow/mini-meditation-let-go/10639456.

LETTING GO WITH BOUNDARIES

Letting go of our past, of expectations, of our attachments and aversions, doesn't give a free pass to anyone to treat us how they want. We don't become doormats, nor do we let energy vampires steal our precious vitality. To be able to let go, we may need to put firm boundaries in place. According to Pema Chödrön in her book *Don't Bite the Hook*:

> Fear, anger, and hatred, while negative emotions, exist to teach us something. When we become aware of our various emotions, we learn why we feel the way we do. When we learn why we feel the way we do, our emotions become productive, rather than destructive forces. Anger usually appears when we fail to set healthy boundaries. If we don't recognize

> what our anger is trying to tell us (the wisdom of our anger), it soon descends into violence, hatred, fear, and destruction.

When I spoke to Mai Elbasandili about boundaries, she said they are crucial. She told me that forgiveness is a fundamental aspect of Islam, deeply rooted in the teachings of the Qur'an. Almost all the surahs (chapters) in the Qur'an start with 'In the name of Allah, the Most Gracious, the Most Merciful', underlining the importance of forgiveness for everyone. In Islam, forgiveness is viewed in two ways: God's forgiveness and human forgiveness.

Islam encourages forgiveness among humans. Allah promises to forgive those who forgive others and to bestow mercy upon them. This belief, deeply embedded in Islamic teachings, helps motivate letting go of resentment and forgiving those who have wronged us. For those who are repeatedly hurt by someone, though, Mai advises that while forgiveness is important, it's also essential to establish boundaries: 'Don't focus on, don't give your energy to these people who harmed you. Just put boundaries up for them. Go away. Leave. Don't stay with them. Move on with your life. Let it go, let it go from your heart.'

CHOOSING WHO WE KEEP IN OUR HEART

What I love the most about this idea is that sometimes we need distance from someone to feel psychologically and physically safe. Once we are free from harm, we should let them go from our hearts.

When my son G was little, he went through a phase of being terrified that I was going to die. I didn't lie to him; I told him one day I would, but most likely not for a very long time. But, I said, no matter what, no matter where I was, alive or not, I was always in his heart. I told him that all the people he loved, and who loved him, were in his heart, especially those we lose. He momentarily looked frightened. 'Where do they all fit? What if I run out of space before you die?'

I explained that our hearts are limitless and just keep stretching like big rubber bands to fit as many people as we love. He breathed a little sigh of relief.

When my beloved grandpa passed away G put his little hand on my heart and said, 'Don't worry, Mummy, he's in here now.'

Now it's not that I don't believe we can't keep the whole world in our hearts, including those who harm us. In most cases, the rubber band stretches and we can fit a lot. But you get to choose. Sometimes, though, I think they are better left out of your beautiful beating centre.

Set a boundary, let them go and make space for someone else – someone who loves you – to squeeze into your boundless love hub.

BOUNDARIES AND DIVORCE

Family lawyer Sarah Swan observes that establishing clear boundaries is essential for enabling the safety and well-being of individuals, allowing them to let go and move on.

She shared a recent example where setting boundaries was crucial for a client's well-being during a divorce. Her client was overwhelmed and stressed by ongoing verbal aggression from her ex-husband and the frequent (several times a day) antagonistic emails and texts she received. This barrage of hostile communication had left her in a state of anxiety, terrified of receiving any emails, making it nearly impossible for her to get through the day let alone find a way to move forward.

To address this, Sarah helped establish firm boundaries regarding when and how communication could occur, and on which platform. By codifying these boundaries through the legal process, this mum was able to escape the fight-or-flight response that had been dominating her life. With these protective measures in place, she could finally breathe, begin to heal and work towards forgiveness. This shift allowed her to focus on fostering a healthier dynamic and relationship within her family, no matter the challenges that came her way.

There are many extreme cases where an even higher boundary needs to be established for the safety of parents and children. But Sarah finds it's often about setting small boundaries to take the heat out of the dynamic and give everyone space to let go and move forward.

IMMIGRATION – THE ULTIMATE LETTING GO

During my tea date with Nasim, she tells me she views immigration as the ultimate letting go with physical boundaries. She sees it as an act of forgiveness for the harm that immigrants receive from the country of their birth. For many people she knows, it's a way to distance themselves from a dangerous place, where their lives were at risk. Instead, they go somewhere they can forget the trauma they left behind and find the safety and future they wouldn't have had if they had stayed. She admits that even with this often huge, geographic boundary, it's sometimes impossible to completely forgive and forget. But for many immigrants who have to let go of their past, the act of forgiveness is their new life.

Letting go may be the ultimate act of forgiveness. But how we do it is dictated by our capacity and circumstances. By not letting things stick and letting go of attachment to our big emotions and all the people and things we cling so tightly to, we have a better chance of dropping the heavier things when they land on us. It's not about pushing away painful experiences; rather, it's about leaning into them fully in the moment, not backing out, letting them be seen and heard so they are satisfied and can move on. The more fully we understand how our likes, dislikes, biases and expectations are driving us each day, the easier it'll be for us to take the steering wheel and control the car when a kangaroo leaps in the middle of the road unexpectedly. Life is a highway – that's another nod to the gen Xers out there – and sometimes we need to set a boundary; lines are marked on the road to keep us safe. The road may be long and winding, but the more familiar we are with it, the more we can crack those windows open, crank the volume and enjoy the road trip.

LETTING GO WITH BOUNDARIES: A SUMMARY

- Healthy boundaries prevent us from being hurt or drained while allowing forgiveness.
- Establishing communication boundaries can help people heal and move forward, especially during difficult family dynamics like divorce.
- You get to choose who to keep in your heart.
- Immigration can be seen as an act of letting go of harm from one's homeland and moving towards a safer future, though complete forgiveness may be difficult.

ONE CONSCIOUS BREATH

Research suggests that it takes somewhere between three and seven breaths to move from the sympathetic nervous system, to the parasympathetic state.

EXERCISE

Whenever you feel charged emotions like anger or hatred, try pausing momentarily. Notice where in the body you feel the emotions, maybe as sensations in the belly, chest or somewhere else. Pay attention to how your breath is. Focus all your awareness on your breath, and slowly breathe in, not like you're forcing air into a balloon, rather visualise your body as a container you are slowly expanding. Breathe into the lower belly, side ribs, back ribs, all the way to the top, without force or stress. Then exhale to slowly let the breath out and feel the ribs and belly soften back in. Observe how you feel after one conscious breath. If you have the time, try taking three conscious breaths or even more. When you are finished, observe the mind, body and breath. Perhaps you feel a little more present, maybe the sensations have changed, and the charged emotions have softened. You can find me guiding a five-minute recorded version of this meditation with some classical music underneath at https://www.abc.net.au/listen/programs/classicflow/mini-meditation-conscious-breaths/10706114

COMPASSION AND MERCY

It's a big jump for most of us to go from hurt and resentment to compassion and mercy. But Buddhism, Hinduism, yoga, modern psychology, family law, Indigenous wisdom and the ancient Greeks suggest it's fundamental to our growth and inner peace, and they offer ways we can do it.

Bob Enright, a psychologist at the University of Wisconsin, Madison, who pioneered the study of forgiveness three decades ago, says true forgiveness goes beyond letting go. He says that offering something positive like empathy, compassion or understanding towards the person that hurt you is the element that makes forgiveness truly powerful. These are the qualities of mercy, which comes back to the idea of kharizomai, the third Greek verb used to describe forgiveness in the Bible, which we touched on earlier.

One of the foundations of yoga and Buddhism is 'ahimsa' or non-harm. It is simply doing our best to not cause harm in the world. According to many religions and spiritual traditions, compassion is the key to everything. It softens the hardest heart and leads to understanding. It is a generous act we can consciously do every day, and it's one of the most important practices when we are working on forgiveness.

To keep compassion front of mind in my daily life, I have a mantra stuck on my fridge. I say it all the time, so a beloved student painted it for me. It's the question I ask whenever I'm in doubt, especially when I'm upset or triggered and I don't know what to do. It is this: 'What would love do?'

Aboriginal Elder Aunty Munya Andrews tells me there is a Kriol word, 'pubella,' that expresses the heart of forgiveness, which she believes lies in compassion. It gets us to the same place my mantra does – from thinking about ourselves to thinking about someone else:

> Back home, in the Kimberley where I come from, we use 'pubella', a corruption of the English words, 'poor fella'; that's really what's at the heart of it. For me, it's this great compassion. I think as Aboriginal

> people, we are the most compassionate people in the world. We could teach the Dalai Lama something about forgiveness, and I love that about my mob. It's intrinsic to us and to our culture. We feel sorry for Country, we feel sorry for Land, we go straight to that place of pubella. Then you're immediately taken out of yourself and you're thinking about the other person.

CURIOSITY

Seeking to understand requires curiosity and compassion. When we sit in judgement, we are viewing the world through the filters of our experience. The mind doesn't see things as they are but through the smudged glasses of our unique world view. When we stay curious and present, we clean the lenses and see things more clearly.

Princeton psychologists Janine Willis and Alexander Todorov found in their research that it takes about one tenth of a second to form an impression of someone. We are constantly unconsciously scanning for threats, which is necessary for survival. But if the mind stays in the loop of our opinions and judgements, we see threats where they don't exist. The more open we stay the more interested we are in others and the easier it is to forgive.

When we put ourselves in others' shoes, we are trying on compassion for size. We don't need to fully comprehend someone else's behaviour. Seeking to understand automatically takes us from judgement to curiosity. We may even start to understand a small part of a person or situation we would have stayed blind to, or discover that an aspect we despise in someone else is also in us.

Very few people wake up in the morning thinking, 'Today I'm going to cause harm!' And yet we all cause harm regularly and unintentionally. It's a great reason for us to stay conscious and minimise the suffering we cause in the world, both to ourselves and others. Instead of judging, we could contemplate our own actions and examine where we cause harm each day. Is there a place we can take conscious action, do better, forgive ourselves or apologise to someone?

Good intent isn't being a pushover; it just reframes how we view the world and how we may go into conversations and experiences with a more open mind.

MAITRI

In Buddhism, the term 'maitri' or 'metta' means friendliness, benevolence, loving kindness, amity, goodwill and active interest in others. It's a key principle of Buddhism and the first of the Four Immeasurables, or limitless qualities, which have no measure or bounds. Buddhists believe these qualities dissolve the boundaries that limit or constrain our experience of the world. In other words, showing these qualities towards ourselves and others can melt the division we create in our lives.

Maitri has a relationship with the other three limitless qualities, which are compassion, joy and equanimity. Pema Chödrön describes maitri as the basis for compassion and the seed for happiness. If you want more happiness in your life, you must have a relationship with friendliness. Ultimately, it starts with you. At the centre of maitri is unconditional, non-judgemental acceptance and love of the self. Once you become friends with and accept yourself, you are naturally kinder to others.

Maitri is also a primary concept of yoga. In the *Yoga Sutras*, it is one of the four keys, or qualities, Patanjali offers to unlock the obstacles of the mind. He suggests that to preserve the serenity of our mind, we should be happy for those who are happy, compassionate to those who are unhappy, delighted for the virtuous, and neutral to those we perceive as being wicked.

NEUTRALITY TO WICKEDNESS

The fourth key is the one that gets a bit hairy when it comes to forgiveness. Patanjali asks us to practise being neutral or indifferent towards those we perceive as wicked. There's nothing passive about neutrality or equanimity in yoga. Staying neutral towards those we see as 'bad' doesn't mean we don't have boundaries or take action. If we see wrong in the world, it's our job, of course, to right it, like all the great yogis (such as Martin Luther King Jr and Gandhi). But the key is to act from a neutral mind. We need to make sure we are not perceiving someone as evil because of the smudgy lenses we view the world through. As the neuroscience has shown us, the only thing that gets disturbed when we stew on the wrongdoing of others is our own mind.

The Gita also encourages neutrality: 'The yogis look upon all – well-wishers, friends, foes, the pious, and the sinners – with an impartial intellect. The yogi who is of equal intellect toward friend, companion, and foe, neutral among enemies and relatives, and unbiased between the righteous and sinful, is considered to be distinguished among humans.'

Sarah Swan has emphasised the crucial role of compassion in divorce and family law, explaining how it can radically change outcomes. The more compassion she brings to the process – not just for her client but also for the opposing party – the better she can understand the underlying pain points causing friction. By deeply understanding the pain both parties are experiencing, Swan can facilitate a process where both individuals feel seen and heard, and where both need to compromise, which is essential for moving forward.

MERCY

Mercy is defined by the *Merriam-Webster Dictionary* as; 'compassion or forbearance shown especially to an offender or to one subject to one's power, a blessing that is an act of divine favour or compassion, or compassionate treatment of those in distress'. As we discovered earlier, the third verb to describe forgiveness in the Bible is kharizomai, which embodies the concept of mercy and comes from 'kharis' or grace. The *Oxford English Dictionary* says grace is 'a quality possessed by human beings: benevolent divine influence regarded as an enduring force in the individual human, having its seat in the soul.' And mercy is often associated with clemency, which the *Merriam-Webster Dictionary* defines as 'a disposition to show kindness or compassion'. Mercy is not giving up or letting go. It's a generosity beyond simply giving. It is connected to a force greater than our individual mortal selves, being steeped in our virtue, and compassionately asking what love would do.

In ancient Greece, the goddesses of mercy were among the most revered and emulated. The goddess Eleos or Elea was the personification of mercy, clemency, compassion and pity. Pausanias was a Greek traveller and geographer, famous for his book *Description of Greece*, which described ancient Greece from his observations. He described Eleos as 'among all the gods the most useful to human life in all its vicissitudes'. Eleos' Roman counterpart, Clementia, was equally important. Her symbols are the branch (possibly the olive tree) and a sceptre (a symbol of power and good governance), and she is often seen leaning against a pillar, column or wall (to indicate stability/strength). She was invoked regularly by leaders who would ask for her help in allowing them to forgive others and give them the strength to show mercy. She was also associated with Julius Caesar due to his legacy as a merciful leader.

Adam Drake, or Drakey, is the founder of Balanced Choice, a program that uses hope theory, fitness and theatre to align the mind, body and spirit so that people can be the best version of themselves. It began in the youth justice space and has already had a profound impact.

When he first started it in 2014, Drakey was going into prisons in the Northern Territory to work with juveniles in detention. He was hell-bent on convincing the government to let him try Balanced Choice with youth in detention.

His enthusiasm and zeal worked a charm on those who had the authority to let him give the program a crack. Since then, Balanced Choice has been hugely successful and he now has a team of other leaders helping him facilitate the program.

Drakey says: 'It's one thing to forgive yourself and even others, but you need to go even further – go to mercy. There's still attachment in forgiveness. Mercy is the next level. Instead of pointing out the wrongs and saying 'you're forgiven', mercy is saying, 'Let's go celebrate the wonderful person you are. Let's move on.' It's like, whoa, that's a different story. It's the ability to stand in awe of what others have been through. The people I work with carry so much in their lives and have had to do way more than I could have ever done in my life. Some of these kids have grown up in my worst nightmare, and they are still able to be where they are today – to still be alive. That's huge.'

COMPASSION AND MERCY: A SUMMARY

- Ahimsa encourages non-harm and understanding.
- Pubella highlights compassion and empathy, focusing on the experiences of others.
- Staying curious about others helps to dissolve judgement and foster compassion.
- Assume people are doing their best.
- Maitri, or unconditional friendliness, fosters love towards oneself and others.
- Practising impartiality towards those perceived as wrongdoers allows for clear action without personal bias.
- Understanding underlying emotional needs in conflict situations leads to better resolutions and healing.
- The Greek and Roman goddesses of mercy symbolise compassion and can be invoked for guidance when forgiving others.
- Mercy goes beyond forgiveness and involves celebrating others' strengths and resilience, and acknowledging their struggles.

GRATITUDE

A gratitude practice can interrupt negative thoughts, like resentment or sadness and replace them with dopamine and serotonin, giving our brain all the feel-good chemicals we need. When we are grateful for what we have, we are more content and can widen our circle of compassion.

EXERCISE

Choose a comfortable seat. Take a moment to bring your awareness into your physical body, noticing how the body, mind and breath feel. Shift your attention back to your physical body and into the space around your heart. How does the heart space feel? Notice any sensations, any pulsations. Shift your focus to the breath. Pay attention to the inhale and the exhale. Don't modify the breath in any way. Allow it to be natural, moving of its own accord.

As you inhale, think of the word 'thanks' or 'gratitude'. As you exhale, think of the name of someone you love. Maybe picture them happy and free. Send them love and gratitude. Start with those close to you, then move to the next person, and the next, noticing the circle widen. Don't be surprised if people arise that you don't expect. Send them gratitude or love and move on. Inhale gratitude, exhale the name or face of someone who pops into your mind. Sit for five minutes or as long as you have. Let go of the gratitude practice. Notice your breath. Shift all of your awareness, all of your focus, back into the heart space. How does it feel?

CANCELLING A DEBT

Anyone who has ever had a bully can attest to the gut-wrenching suffering they bring. Most of us have profoundly wounding memories of being bullied by someone at some point in our lives. And we've all been perpetrators too. It takes a lot to forgive ourselves and others, especially when the consequences of bullying can last a lifetime – or even take someone's life. But what the research shows is that holding on to our grudges is only going to keep us stuck and impact our wellbeing. And if we can find a way to get over our grudges and erase the debt, we can start fresh, with a joyful future ahead of us.

As discussed earlier, the idea of forgiveness in the context of cancelling a debt comes from the Greek verb used in the Bible, 'aphiemi'. Aphiemi is wiping the slate clean as though it didn't happen. The thought of letting bullies off the hook in this way, cancelling their debt as if they didn't try to break you, can feel like an unreasonable ask. And yet for many people it has been profoundly liberating for them to do so and the key to moving forward.

When we hold grudges towards those who hurt us, the mind keeps circling back to the wrongdoing again and again. And, as stated previously, this kind of rumination ends up hardwiring our brain like frozen circuits. In a report by Ash Fisher and Danielle Wade for *Psych Central*, they examine the existing research around holding grudges and expound upon how detrimental this kind of rumination is to our physical and mental health, especially in increasing blood pressure and impacting heart health and cognitive functioning. It can even trigger violent or aggressive behaviours and bring substantial life challenges.

The problem is that just like the bullied mouse friend we spoke about earlier, when repeatedly bullied, a mouse will stay in the fight-or-flight state even after the bully has been removed. This same phenomenon, of getting stuck in fight or flight after repeated stress, is seen in many studies, including research on physiology and the stress response by Brianna Chu and colleagues. Their work showed that when stressful events persist for extended periods of time, the body adapts to cope with these higher stress levels. It secretes stress hormones to maintain this new norm of elevated stress that it gets used to, which can result in many long-term effects, including burnout, irritability, frustration, anxiety and depression.

We see this illustrated in the 2020 report *Australia's Children* from the Australian Institute of Health and Welfare, which shows bullying has a wide range of physical, psychological, social, emotional and academic consequences for kids. They are more likely to have poor academic performance, struggle with transition points throughout life, have mental health concerns, such as feelings of anxiety and depression, and be at higher risk of suicide. It has only gotten worse over time with the rise of cyberbullying, giving victims no respite from their abusers.

One person who is well placed to talk about feeling the impact of bullies, even long after they have been removed, is Matthew Backer. I met Matt at *Play School*, where we have both been presenters for over a decade. Matt is eternally playful, bringing seemingly boundless energy to everything he does. This makes him one of those people you just want to be around. I know we will find moments of joy and mischief that otherwise wouldn't have been in the episode, which is why it's so heartbreaking to imagine what would have happened if his school bullies, who tried so hard to beat that light out of him, had won.

Matt and I have spoken about his many years of being bullied at high school, and the profound impact it had on his life. He had a joyous primary school life. Unsurprisingly, he was the school captain and the fun guy of the school, and he got along with everyone. When he arrived at high school, it was a huge shock to the system. An all-boys Catholic school in Brisbane was not kind to the small, unathletic boy who stood out like a sore thumb. He was bullied daily, relentlessly, for five years. It nearly broke him and left him with long-term anger that was impossible to shake:

> Growing up, I held a lot of anger at the loss of that young boy, because it's such a formative time, and when you're told every day for five years that what you are is, like, disgusting or wrong or sinful, when you don't even know who you are, you really start to lose a big part of yourself. And I think that's the main thing that I sort of struggled to forgive and accept. I didn't really know who I was, and then I stayed in the closet a lot longer because of it, and

> then I became an actor in an industry that doesn't champion gay actors at all. So I got to my late 20s and realised I was having panic attacks and weird reactions to things that shouldn't matter, and stressing over things that I didn't need to stress about. But I reached thirty and realised, like, I didn't know who I was. That's the anger that I probably held on to the most.

SHORT-TERM ANGER

Initially, Matt needed to hold onto his anger to stay strong enough to weather the punches coming his way. Part of this is the power of acknowledging his feelings. But the other part illustrates how we desperately look for solid ground when we are vulnerable and groundless. This is akin to what Pema Chödrön says about kleshas. We get hooked by them because they can give us a sense of power, a sense of something solid to hold on to. Matt says:

> On the one hand, holding a grudge makes me angry, short-tempered, my energy feels off, and that's not a good place to be. But sometimes it makes me feel strong, which I think I needed to have in high

school. There was no way I would have survived five years without that. No way. So, it's a double-edged sword. That's the same with forgiving. If someone hurts you, it doesn't help you if you're holding a grudge against them while they're off living their life. It just makes you sort of sad in your bed, when you should be living your life. But on the other hand, it does make you strong as well. Because you acknowledge: hey, no, my feelings are valid! They hurt me! On one hand, it can damage you, and on the other hand, it can actually make you really strong.

RESPITE, FRIENDS, STORIES AND COMEDY

Three things that got him through those years were horror movies, TV shows and his best friends. There were no mobile phones or social media, so the bullying would stop on weekends.

Matt and his friends would lock themselves away, watching horror movies and *Buffy the Vampire Slayer* (oh, how I longed to be Sarah Michelle Gellar), finding solace in stories of strong women overcoming fear. They'd watch these resilient girls go head-to-head against vampires and masked men terrorising them, but they'd always win in the end. Through stories, they were given examples of how, even through oppression, you can come out the other side. The other medicine was laughter:

> For so long in high school, it was so hard, so shit, and comedy for me was a bit of relief ... if I could make someone laugh, they'd think I was okay. It's a defence mechanism, still, because if I can, I'll make a joke ... every five seconds. That's why I love *Play School*. I love clowning, I love trying to find the joke, I love trying to work out what will make someone laugh. If I can make someone laugh, we're good.

TIME HEALS ALL WOUNDS

Now, approaching 40, he says that time and distance have helped him get past his grudges towards those who made his life unbearable for so long. He didn't consciously cancel the debt. It just happened as he grew up and found himself as an actor. The sense of self they had destroyed finally started to form again, on his own terms. With a stronger sense of who he was, his values, his worth and his purpose as a storyteller, the debt was eventually cancelled with grace. He also realised they were just young people growing up in their own imperfect way:

> I think that's probably what has helped the most. I don't expect any of them to apologise. Because I look back and go, 'We were so young.' … It's about seeing people and going, 'Oh, we all make bad decisions.' We must be open to the idea that people can change. I don't hold any grudges, and I don't expect anyone from high school to have to say sorry. That's not where I am anymore.

USING STORYTELLING TO FORGIVE

With his passion for comedy and horror, Matt came up with an idea for a short film, *Die Bully Die*. It is centred around hero character Max imagining all the possible ways his former bully might die. It sprang from a real place, rooted in the dark thoughts he used to have about his bullies. But placed in the comedy and horror genre, it's a powerful exploration of forgiving our bullies and freeing them from the debt they owe us.

In the film, Matt explores the struggle of wanting to see

his bullies as villains but recognising they are just imperfect beings, that some people can and do change. 'And that's what the film is,' says Matt. 'We're so adamant that Drew's character, Adam, [the bully] is a lovely, kind, funny man. That's the struggle for Max. He wants his bullies to still be the villains from his teenage years because it's easier to hold on to a grudge that way.'

The process of making the film deepened Matt's desire to forgive completely, let go and cancel any last remnants of what he felt was owed to the young boy who was squashed. He also realised that holding onto anger only hurt himself. But like Nasim, it made me think that perhaps forgiveness can't be rushed. Rather, it comes slowly, in stages and layers. And whether it's as long as an epic novel or a never-ending story ... it can start with a powerful short film.

CANCELLING THE MOST UNFORGIVABLE DEBT

Intuitive healer Simi Koster and I met through a mutual friend when she came to a book club event at Gertrude & Alice Bookstore in Bondi. She is one of those people who is completely present, seeing right through you with compassion and humour. You can tell she's not sitting on the surface of life; she's living it all. After connecting over writing and stories, she sent me a link to a piece she wrote called *Legacy*, her personal account of life as a survivor.

In the piece, Simi describes growing up in an abusive home, enduring frequent physical and emotional mistreatment from her mum. So, on a mundane Monday afternoon, over chai and chocolate brownies, we meet to discuss her extraordinary journey:

> I could never do things right, nothing was perfect in her eyes; spilling milk, taking an extra bit of food from the fridge or asking friends over to my house were all no-noes. Her constant hand on the trigger to act aggressively towards me was exhausting. That is why I could never concentrate when trying to study at home, I was always nervously on watch, on guard. I would constantly be hiding from my mother, never sure of what mood she would be in after school or after I came home from being at my friend's house, which was my only example of how a family behaved together. I was never sure what would set her off but could just see it in her eyes to prepare for what was to come. Wire coathangers

> were her favourite tool, even now it's hard to have them in my closet. Even with a broken arm in a cast, that slap across the face with the red talons found their mark.

Over the years, Simi has built a life filled with love, with a supportive, devoted husband and two secure, protected children. She has turned her painful past into a foundation for helping others, pursuing a career as a healer and mentor. Through this journey, she learned the power of forgiveness and embraced her inner strength, ultimately breaking the cycle of abuse and creating a life of love and light. Blown away by her story, I ask her how she became this joyful, powerful, engaging human that people are drawn to, including me.

CONNECT TO THINGS THAT SHOW YOU LOVE

Simi tells me she found solace in her cat Beau, her teddies and her best friend's family, who showed her she was valued, lovable and worthy of joy. The light of the full moon provided her with a sense of comfort, safety and guidance during her darkest moments. She often prayed to it, asking for counsel. The moon symbolised a constant source of light and hope, but also change, showing her that the only constant was transformation.

LEAVING THE SITUATION AND SETTING BOUNDARIES

The first thing she did on her road to healing was leave home at seventeen. With no support or contacts, she moved from Brisbane to Sydney to escape the abuse and start a new life. She arrived in Sydney with a suitcase, slept on the floor, ate packet noodles and worked three jobs to survive. Even though her new life was no bed of roses, she was out of survival mode. I tell her it's not always possible for people to set a boundary or get distance like that, and she agrees. But, she says, as best you can, if at all possible, you must get physical distance and take yourself out of the situation. 'When I left Brisbane at seventeen my mother said to me with such venom and cruelty in her voice "you'll be back in six months." I shouldn't laugh, but this was the best motivation to keep me moving forward and to never return. A great catalyst paid forward even after all these years.'

SEEING HER MUM AS IMPERFECT

She knew her mum didn't know any better, which enabled her to feel compassion towards her. From afar, she cancelled the debt completely, which means she forgave her. But more importantly, she also forgave her soul. I'm not sure many people could do that, I tell her, and that's when she echoes what keeps coming up as the most practical piece of forgiveness advice: 'Forgive like a grain of sand. Start somewhere. For it will become a sandstorm.'

HER HUSBAND AND KIDS

She also credits comedy, laughter, ocean swimming and bodyboard surfing year-round as helping her heal. But says her greatest legacy is her kids. The life she got to live, her incredibly loving husband, the mother she got to be – she broke the cycle. It ends with her.

This little bombshell blows my heart out because it takes me back to Agamemnon and how violence usually begets violence in the stories of ancient Greece and Rome, and no one wins. And then you have Simi, who has every reason to hate and seek justice and revenge. But instead, she chooses love. And everyone wins. She freed herself, she freed her Mum, but more importantly, she freed her kids. And in this moment, I finally understand a little corner of forgiveness, like a grain of sand one day becoming a sandstorm.

CANCELLING A DEBT: A SUMMARY

- Holding grudges is like carrying an unresolved debt – it keeps us stuck like the bullied mouse.
- While anger may provide short-term strength, it can turn into a burden.
- Recognising that bullies and abusers are imperfect people helps to cancel their debt.
- Using storytelling helps process pain.
- In cases like Simi's, cancelling the debt of her mother's abuse allowed her to break the cycle of violence.
- Forgiveness is like a grain of sand; it eventually becomes a sandstorm.

SIMPLE MINDFULNESS PRACTICE

Mindfulness is not about suppressing or changing big emotions. It is learning to see them for what they are; transient feelings that will rise and fall, like waves on an ocean. We identify them, acknowledge them, and allow them to wash away. The ocean will always be there, but we can learn to surf instead of being pulled under the current. Neuroanatomist Jill Bolte Taylor says that most emotions don't last longer than 90 seconds. If we can sit with big emotions for 90 seconds, instead of backing away, they will pass. This mindfulness practice allows us to practise exactly this.

EXERCISE

When you experience a big emotion, sit down in a quiet place. Notice your breath. Is it long or short? Witness it first, then take gentle, slow breaths. If you feel triggered, a great way to get out of the fight-or-flight response is to slow the breath down or breathe into your lower belly, which connects us to the parasympathetic nervous system. Place your hands on your lower belly and see if you can consciously send more breath there.

Observe how your body feels. Where in the body do you feel the emotions? Is there tension, heat or shakiness? Get curious.

As feelings bubble to the surface, acknowledge and meet each one with compassion and presence. You can even verbally do so. If you see anger arise, acknowledge it and say, 'I see you, anger.' Don't try to judge or change it. Let it be. Allow it to rise like a wave, and then let it wash away.

Allow the practice to widen your circle of compassion, as you contemplate how we all feel these big emotions. It's a shared experience in life. Let this broaden your tolerance, perhaps softening your judgement the next time someone has a big feeling like anger or sadness.

HOLDING ON TO WHO YOU ARE

From Islam to Hinduism, from surviving a marital affair to being wrongly accused of infanticide, the Stoic perspective of holding on to who we are is often the key to our inner peace. We cannot control others, but we can control how we respond to them. And the stories and teachings below provide the insight and wisdom of how we can bring this into our own lives.

STAYING NEUTRAL TO AVOID FURTHER SUFFERING

Like Socrates, another Stoic, Marcus Aurelius, often spoke of the importance of holding on to who we are and focusing on our virtue. He says, 'The best way to avenge yourself is to not be like that.'

Late in his reign, he learned that his trusted general, Avidius Cassius, believing Aurelius was seriously ill, had revolted in Syria. Aurelius didn't react with anger but kept the news secret, hoping Cassius would come to his senses. When he didn't, Aurelius prepared to march against him but announced his intention to capture and forgive him. He stated that he hoped Cassius would not be killed or commit suicide so he could show mercy. Unfortunately, Cassius was assassinated by a soldier before they could meet. Aurelius refused to execute any of Cassius's supporters and urged the Roman Senate to avoid further bloodshed, embodying the Stoic principles of forgiveness, self-control and understanding.

MAINTAINING YOUR INTEGRITY

When my girlfriend chose to stay and fight for her marriage, the thing she was most proud of was how she held herself throughout the whole process. The path to reconciliation was extremely difficult, and even though there was nothing solid to hold on to, the one thing she could do was hold on to her values. She did everything she could to stay true to herself and own the parts of the relationship dynamic that were hers, ensuring he eventually did the same. Today, they have a robust, healthy marriage, and when she looks back, she can see the affair was not about her. It was about him. It was his issues, which are not, and never were, a reflection on her. Her ability to maintain her ethics and principles not only helped her heal but also became a source of great inner strength.

DHARMA – DUTY AND PURPOSE

Seema tells me that if you live your dharma, which is your purpose and duty, there will never be anything to forgive. I suspect this is similar to the Stoic perspective on staying true to your virtue, so I ask her what she means and how we know if we are living our dharma:

> Dharma means that if I'm a mother, I have to do all my dharma. Being a wife, being a sister, being a friend, these are all my duties. And I have to fulfil those properly. So first come the house duties, then social duties, with my friends, with people abroad, with somebody coming to my door and asking for something. I mean, dharma is always defined as what is righteous. And you believe that if you're really on a path and you do a lot of prayers and chanting and spiritual practices, your inner voice tells you. It is

> when you're confused in your mind with all kinds of emotions and negative feelings, or even positive feelings ... if too much is going on in your mind, you're not able to hear your inner voice. So, to clear all that clutter, all that chattering in your mind, you need the practices. And once it is clear, then you can very clearly understand. ... It's like somebody directing you, do this and don't do this. You see that whenever you're cleaning pots. You clean it from inside. Outside also, but most of it is inside. You basically want to clean more inside.

I think about how many of us are concerned with cleaning the outside of our pots, making sure everything looks squeaky clean. It's such a good reminder that no amount of time is ever wasted when we clean the inside of our pots. When we do the things that keep us calm, centred and clear. Whether it's meditating, breath practices, singing, swimming or surfing, prioritising mental space will help us get clear on what's important, and then, according to Seema, there's nothing really to forgive. When we have mental space and clarity, we will be able to hear our inner voice, and it will know exactly what to do. And know how we should be spending every precious moment of our lives.

YOUR PURPOSE AND PURIFYING YOUR HEART

During our meeting, Mai told me about the story of the Prophet Joseph. Even though his brothers tried to kill him when he finally encountered them years later in Egypt, he didn't punish them; he forgave them. She believes that this kind of forgiveness is a deliberate choice. By purifying the heart of anger, jealousy and other negative emotions, you can focus more clearly on what truly matters. She says that holding onto anger only keeps it at the forefront of your mind, preventing any progress in your life. Instead, you need to focus on the most important aspects of your life and move forward with a clear and unburdened heart.

LOOSENING THE GRIP

One of the yamas (ethical practices) Patanjali suggests in the *Yoga Sutras* is 'aparigraha' (non-possessiveness/non-grasping). When we stop holding on to things so tightly, he says, we understand our purpose in this precious life. It requires a lot of energy to hold on to resentment, and as we loosen that grip, we can shift our efforts to the important things in life. We cannot forgive without loosening our grip. It's not possible.

Think about how much time we spend obsessing when we feel hatred instead of focusing our attention on what we should be doing with our own lives. Instead of stalking your ex's Instagram, spend those extra minutes in meditation, going for a walk or updating your resume. Do the things that will get you the life, and partner, that is aligned with who you are.

CELTIC MYTHOLOGY – GRACE

My grandmother was Irish and I have a love for all things Celtic, including some of their myths. Rhiannon is a major figure in Welsh and Celtic mythology, an ethereal and striking goddess who wore gold silk and rode a shining white horse. Though two men vied for her love, she married a mortal prince, Pwyll, and had a baby boy. Tragically, the newborn disappeared the night of his birth and her six sleepy maids, fearing retribution for their error, killed a puppy and smeared blood on Rhiannon's mouth and face. She was accused of infanticide and cannibalism, and although her life was spared, Pwyll didn't cast her out; she had to do her penance instead.

She was condemned to sit at the gate of the castle and carry visitors in on her back, just like her shining white horse, which she readily agreed to. She understood that this was her fate, no matter how just or unjust it was. For some time, she bore the burden of a crime she didn't commit. No drama – just dharma.

But her son, Pryderi, was not dead. He was kidnapped by a spectral creature who was later defeated by a horse lord. As the child grew, the horse lord saw his resemblance to Prince Pwyll, having once been his courtier, and so Rhiannon was finally reunited with her son. Everyone rejoiced at her innocence, and she didn't seek vengeance or revenge.

The horse-like grace, steadiness and strength of Rhiannon illustrates again that forgiveness is not about what others do to you, it's about how you respond. Graceful and steady wins the race.

HOLDING TO YOUR FAITH NO MATTER WHAT

May Samali is the founder and CEO of Human Leadership Lab, a global leadership development company. She is also a speaker, facilitator, coach, researcher, investor and board director, and a Fellow at the Institute of Coaching at Harvard Medical School. May and I met recently and have forged a fast, firm friendship based on long walks and conversations that unpack the world. She is an inspiring, smart human, and when I hear about her grandpa's story, it's no surprise why.

In 1979, during the Islamic Revolution in Iran, the Shah was overthrown and an Islamic regime took power. As a result, religious minorities, including Zoroastrians, Jews, Christians and Baha'is, began facing systematic persecution. The Baha'i Faith, which emerged after Islam, was not recognised as a legitimate religion in the Iranian constitution. Baha'is were regarded as infidels, and many were targeted, arrested and martyred for their beliefs.

May's maternal grandpa, Hossein Lamè, was among the Baha'is who were active in their faith, engaging in projects with young people, arts and socio-economic development. On 13 February 1984, he was captured by Iranian authorities, along with eight other senior members of the Baha'i community in his neighborhood in Tehran:

> He was taken away, and for those first few days and weeks, his family didn't know if he was dead or alive. The odds are, you expect that they're never going

> to come back, but they ended up putting them in prison. For the first six months he was in solitary confinement. There was a little window at the top of his cell, but the length of his prison cell was shorter than his body, so he was just curled up. There was just a little toilet inside and a ripped straw blanket to sleep on … and that's all he had. And no contact with the outside world … I remember COVID … And how difficult it was, that isolation, for me, but I had a big house. So, I can't fathom that. But that's how it all began …

He remained in prison for five years and twenty-three days, from 1984 to 1989. His imprisonment was solely because of his Baha'i faith and his refusal to deny it. One of the core principles of the Baha'i Faith is that you do not recant your beliefs. Despite the physical and emotional pain, May's grandpa never wavered. There was a lot of emotional pain, a lot of physical persecution and cruelty. He was beaten, sometimes with a metal stapler, and blindfolded during interrogations so he never knew when the next blow would come. He endured repeated interrogations, yet he never gave up the names of other Baha'is or compromised his faith. While he was there, 10 of his 17 Baha'i cellmates were martyred:

> Through the latter years he was eventually allowed to write short letters. They were scratched on the back of scrap paper and my grandma would collect them when visiting him. When he was eventually released from prison, he documented his experiences in letters he sent to his children for safekeeping. But we could never trust that the letters would make it out of Iran, so he would write the first page of the letter and send it to my aunty, send the second page to my mum, and then the sisters would piece the letter together. In those letters, he wasn't talking about what was happening that was bad. He was wanting to send love, or he would have dreams about one of them being pregnant (which was always true).

When May met her grandpa for the first time at the age of eight, she never heard him speak of his suffering. He chose not to dwell on the past or share details of his persecution. May learned many lessons from her grandpa's capacity to forgive and let go, even in the most heinous conditions.

He was steadfast in his faith, enduring unimaginable hardships with resilience and hope. He always found the good, even after his release, and held on to gratitude for the smallest blessings; a glimmer of light, visits with his wife, or the chance to write after years of captivity. He had courage to stand by his values, even in the face of violence, and was unwavering. He saw the bigger picture, refusing to take his suffering personally, and viewed his captors as people following orders, not inherently bad. Believing his persecution was part of a greater plan to reveal truths about humanity, he separated the policies of the government from his love for his country and the goodness of people from their actions and never criticised the Iranian government despite all they did to him. May believes it was all of this that meant he could be free, both in and out of prison.

> All my memories of this man is that he was the most gentle, loving person. He was an accountant by profession, worked in a local hospital, and so poetic ... I get a lot of my creative side from him. He never said anything bad about the Iranian government – ever. My dad has ten hours of recordings of

> him speaking about everything. There's not one mention of pointing blame. And that meant he could tread with lightness. He didn't carry the burden. And you could sense it, this man that was really at peace and free.

TESTING YOUR CORE VALUES

When running her own company and helping CEOs grapple with difficult decisions and tricky scenarios, May has always seen personal leadership as moving towards your north star, your core values:

> When I think about the example of my grandpa, in one way it would have been easy for him to recant his faith to be freed from prison. But his values were tested. It's easy and convenient to say, 'These are my core values', but we only realise the power of them when they're tested. For leadership, your values aren't meant to feel good all the time. They're meant to provide you with a direction when things are hard. Those are the moments we need to go back to the core of what we've said is most important to us and stick by it.

HOLDING ON TO WHO YOU ARE: A SUMMARY

- Focus on your own integrity rather than letting others' actions define you.
- Living in alignment with your dharma, personal duties and purpose removes the need for forgiveness.
- We waste energy holding on to resentment. Releasing the grip on past grievances allows us to focus on our own growth and purpose.
- Forgiveness and grace come not from others' actions but from how we choose to respond.
- True leadership and personal strength come from staying true to one's core values, even when they are tested in difficult circumstances.
- Focusing on small moments of gratitude helps build resilience and maintain a positive outlook, even in challenging situations.
- Being able to forgive and separate people's actions from their inherent goodness allows for emotional freedom and lightness.
- Leadership involves courage, particularly when values are challenged. It's in those moments that conviction grows, and true personal leadership is demonstrated.

MINDFUL WALKING

While mindful walking has no single definition, the idea is to focus your awareness while moving through your environment. Here is an exercise to help you do that.

EXERCISE

Take a walk in your neighbourhood. Notice the way your body moves you walk. Your posture, the ground beneath your feet, your body weight, the shoes you're wearing. Notice your foot lifting and how it rolls from heel to toe. Try to keep the spine long and the shoulders and face relaxed. Feel which muscles the body is using and notice your arms naturally swinging along. Become aware of your surroundings with an open mind and curiosity. See the colours, shapes and visuals of the world around you. Feel the sun or breeze on your face. Notice the smells, tastes, sounds and sensations on the body. Focus on the breath. Allow it to move naturally with your walking rhythm, ensuring it is easy and free. Watch how the breath flows and changes. As the mind starts to wander, notice where it's gone, acknowledge the thought, and come back to focusing on the breath. Use the breath as an anchor to keep coming back to if the mind wanders, or shift your attention between all the senses.

DISTURBING THE CHEMISTRY

When it comes to forgiveness, we have seen in previous chapters that the mind and body are intrinsically linked, so when we don't forgive, our physical and mental health suffer. Energetics and subtle anatomy are concepts that provide models which codify this idea and take it one step further, asserting that understanding how energy functions within our bodies is the critical piece. The subtle body is a concept derived from ancient Indian and Taoist philosophy, which describes the aspects of the human body that are not just the physical – the mental and energetic components. It encompasses the idea that we are fundamentally energy moving through physical form, or as Einstein says, 'Everything is energy, and that's all there is to it.' Rather than solid structures of skin, bone, tissue and organs we can see and dissect, subtle anatomy explores and describes the energetic systems that operate within us. Ancient cultures recognised these systems as infinitely more powerful than just skin and bone. They spoke about how critical managing our energy is, even though each culture may have used different language and models to explain it. Traditional Chinese medicine, Ayurveda, yoga, and even the principles of Kanyini, handed down by Aboriginal elders, all share potent wisdom based on energy lines and how to govern them. This was long before Western medicine was cutting open cadavers to study the physical form. Seema's perspective of forgiveness mirrors what the neuroscience and research have shown us, but instead of physical anatomy, she talks about subtle anatomy.

PRESERVING YOUR CHEMISTRY

Seema tells me forgiveness is all about understanding and preserving our body chemistry, which is totally up to us. No one else can do it. And if we allow someone else to mess up our energy balance, that's on us. She says:

> When you have any grudges, you are more bothering yourself than that person. Because you're always

> carrying it. You have to keep reminding yourself: 'I'm not going to talk to him. I'm angry with him. I'm not going to talk to him. I'm angry. He did this, he did that.' Like that, you're constantly disturbing your body chemistry. Why should I waste my energy on getting angry with somebody, getting upset, and then scolding, or trying to correct him, or trying to teach him a lesson? This is all a waste of time and energy. I want all my feelings to be focused on my inner growth ... I want my chemistry to be flowing, and nice, and clean, and happy hormones. I don't want any disturbing hormones. Yes, I am very careful that I don't want to spoil my chemistry.

The Stoics shared this idea of forgiving others to preserve our body chemistry. Epictetus said in *The Art of Living:* 'Forgive others for their misdeeds over and over again. This gesture fosters inner ease.'

CHINESE MEDICINE

Traditional Chinese medicine (TCM) has a similar perspective on balancing energy, especially when it comes to forgiveness. Its understanding of physiology focuses more on the energetic functions of organs rather than the biological aspects emphasised in Western medicine.

For example, when TCM refers to organs like the kidneys, heart or spleen, it's not discussing them in the same way Western medicine does. Chinese practitioners understand these organs as being responsible for various physical and psychological functions, but not in a strictly anatomical sense. For instance, the kidneys in TCM are seen as the source of 'jing', our reproductive energy and vital fluids. This concept is quite different from the Western view, which sees the kidneys as filtration organs.

In TCM, organs represent broader energy centres, each with specific functions related to the body and the psyche's balance of yin, yang, vital essences and elements. Each organ has an element associated with it. TCM asserts that everything in existence is made up of five elements: water, earth, fire, wood and metal. And the balance of these elements determines our well-being.

Jade Clark is a TCM physician with decades of experience. She trained with the Sydney Institute of Traditional Chinese Medicine and Guangzhou United Family Hospital in South China and is known by all her students and clients as having 'magic hands'. We met when she taught anatomy on my first yoga teacher training many moons ago, and she has become not only a close friend and colleague but also one of the people I rely on to put me back together when I am falling apart.

When I ask her about TCM and forgiveness, she says that when the elements are imbalanced, we can only see ourselves as victims rather than empowered, growing beings, learning what we can from every experience:

> According to Chinese Medicine's wisdom, our ability to forgive demonstrates the quality of the five elements moving through our current state of consciousness. It indicates our understanding of the fundamental reason things happen the way they do and whether our enquiry leads to blame and judgement or wisdom and evolution. If the Wood/Liver energy is imbalanced, we will only see crime. We will only see ourselves as victims blindsided by perpetrators. This desire to feed on injustice prevents the soul from connecting with the wisdom of what the experience was meant to provide. When the Wood energy is balanced, the appropriate state of responsibility is reclaimed, not

> simply of our part to play in all things, but more importantly, by reclaiming our innate responsibility of being the sole determinant of our response at every moment. Liver energy provides the means to self-determine our state despite circumstances, emphasising self-responsibility and moving away from actions requiring forgiveness.

Like Seema, she comes back to the idea of preserving the balance of our energy and chemistry and taking responsibility for it ourselves.

YOGA MODELS OF ENERGETICS

Yoga physiology is the way the body is described and understood according to yogic teachings. It focuses on the subtle body with the understanding that working with energy and subtle anatomy is the most powerful way to ensure our vitality. There are several models that incorporate this integrated understanding that we are all made up of energy. Our thoughts, feelings, physical body, it's all just energy moving through our form. So the models suggest we are made up of mental, energetic and physical tiers that all affect one another. When we don't forgive, we are impacting our whole system, all the different layers. This is why the yogis speak so much about managing our energy through a wholistic lens, through our physical health, thoughts, words and actions. The models are mentioned in early Vedic texts and ancient yogis mapped it all out in some detail. They found that our energy flows throughout the body along little pathways called 'nadis'. This is similar to the idea of energy lines or 'meridians' in TCM.

There are around 72,000 nadis in the body, with three major ones. Sushumna, the central channel, is like the major freeway that sits along the spine. The other two, ida and pingala, start on either side and wind along sushumna. The seven points along the central channel, where the three main ones intersect, are home to the chakras. The chakra system suggests that different energy centres in the body reflect our relative ease or dis-ease in the world as they are the lenses through which we perceive our relationships and everything around us. Each one has a number of things associated with it, such as an element, a sense, and a bija or seed mantra. And each one is associated with a particular relationship. They are like wheels of energy sitting along that freeway. Like all roads, when there are lots of vehicles or there's an obstacle of some sort, the result is a traffic jam.

In the same way, when the chakras are out of balance, energy can't flow freely through the channels and they get blocked. And because the yogic understanding that the energetic, physical and mental tiers all affect one another, this is when dis-ease can turn into disease.

The yogis believed that our life force, our full potential, is dormant, like a sleeping snake at the base of the central channel. When that major freeway is clear, our energy can flow easily up the pathway and we are full of health, ease, vitality and joy, and we can reach our potential. But if there are traffic jams along the way, energy gets stuck, and so do we. When the energy gets stuck, for example through negative thoughts and feelings, life does too.

When the chakras are out of balance, we find ourselves unable to forgive, ruminating, filled with anger and hatred; we are creating a bunch of congestion along that major freeway. Just like much of the scientific research has shown, not forgiving is limiting our potential and creating substantial imbalance in our health and well-being. The first step is to clear the energetic pathway and balance the chakras through yogic practice. But then, the goal is to go further. It's to remember who you are beyond the energetic, mental and physical body you've been given.

The most powerful way to work with forgiveness and the chakras is to connect to that deeper, quieter part of yourself. Beyond the attachments and aversions we talked about in the kleshas, beyond your personality self and everything the world has told you that you are.

Finding moments of stillness at home, or in nature, whether formal meditation and breath practices, or simply being still and quiet for a moment, allows you to feel that part of yourself. That centre is core of who you are, according to yoga, and in that quiet, infinitely powerful place, forgiveness will be more accessible.

KOSHAS

The koshas, or sheaths, provide another subtle anatomy framework for recognising how interconnected different parts of us are. In Vedantic philosophy, it is said that each one of us is an upadhi or container with five different sheaths that are hiding our true or eternal Self. They are like layers of an onion: physical, mental, emotional, energetic and our bliss state. *The Upanishads* first described these five sheaths, and how they are all interconnected. We can see how they all impact one another, for example, when we drain the physical layer by eating badly, not hydrating or exercising, and sleeping poorly. As a result, the mental and energetic layers will be affected and we'll feel sluggish and flat. Conversely, when we feel anger or hatred, we might not nourish the body. Instead of focusing on our positive physical habits like exercising, or nourishing ourselves with healthy food, we may turn to alcohol, drugs, sugar or poor food choices, which impacts the physical layer by making us feel unwell. This then affects the energetic layer, making us feel lethargic. The koshas are constantly in play, either nourishing one another and our overall well-being, or draining us. Similar to working with the chakras, we want to first balance the layers, by purifying the body and mind, but then get beyond them. To remember who you are beyond the physical, energetic and mental sheaths. To see that we get very caught up in things beyond our control, relationships, illness, events. To accept that everything is constantly transient and changing. But according to yoga, there is a fundamental part of you, that energy which is flowing through the universe constantly, that is not subject to change. Again, finding a way to connect to that deeper part of yourself is the antidote to not being able to forgive. Because when we spend more time in the peaceful nature of that place, we get less caught up in the drama of our lives.

Seema explains it in this way:

> Whatever you see, it's just a manifestation of the things in the Supreme Consciousness. The Supreme Consciousness is the only reality. But really, being a Hindu, because we are made of the five elements, all these five koshas. We see the world as very real, which is not real at all. So because we assume it as real, we get entangled in it, and the emotions hit us, and everything is affected. We get affected by it.

VIBRATION

According to quantum theory, matter is made up of particles that rotate at different frequencies, and its essence is energy. From a quantum physics standpoint, all beings are just particles vibrating at certain frequencies. And every vibration is equivalent to a feeling, which can be positive or negative. Because all matter and energy are just vibrating particles, things that we perceive as solid objects are just manifestations of energy vibrating in a particular way. Or, as Einstein says: 'Concerning matter, we have been all wrong. What we have called matter is energy, whose vibration has been so lowered as to be perceptible to the senses. There is no matter.'

Sound waves are also a form of vibration. As molecules bump into each other, vibrating in a particular way, a chain reaction happens where others bump into each other, creating sound waves. So if our ear is in range of a particular vibration, we hear sound. The molecules need to be moving at a certain speed for us to hear them. According to research done at *Science World*, animals can hear higher pitches than us. Cats can hear higher pitches than dogs, and porpoises can hear the fastest vibrations of all, up to 150,000 times per second.

Within the energetic models and this belief that energy is simply vibration, there is also the understanding that sound impacts our well-being. In the chakra system, each energy centre has a bija or seed sound associated with each chakra. For example, the root chakra is the sound 'lam'. Tibetan singing bowls are a type of instrument that have been used for healing and meditation in South-East Asia, by Tibetan and Buddhist monks for centuries. When played, they create long deep, rich tones and sounds. According to a study at the University of California, there are significant beneficial effects of Tibetan singing bowl meditations on a number of markers related to well-being.

OM AND CHANTING

Shaman and sound healer Gareth Mansell describes om as the 'Great Eraser'. Chanting om can be very powerful in interrupting the circuit, changing the station and resetting the nervous system. According to the Vedas, om represents and symbolises many things, and throughout the yoga philosophy the potency of om is spoken about often. In the *Yoga Sutras*, om is God, and so making this sound connects you directly to something greater than yourself. With the understanding that everything in the universe is made up of energy and vibration, and sound is the embodiment of that, chanting om allows us to feel that at a cellular level. We all know how it can feel when you're singing in the car or the shower at the top of your little lungs. It helps us connect to a more joyful part of ourselves.

Om is also connected to the Trimurti in yoga, which is the three qualities of creation, sustenance and destruction represented as a triad of deities, Brahma, Vishnu and Shiva. In its essence is the idea that everything in the manifest world moves through cycles of birth, sustaining and ending. Things begin, they endure for a period of time and they end. That's the deal of being alive. Chanting om embodies all three realities, which allows us to work with forgiveness when it comes to endings, destruction and things falling apart. In order to begin again or move on, we need to let things go. Sometimes forgiveness is simply letting the falling apart happen and accepting whatever damage has been done in the process. When we make the sound om, and we get to the end of the sound, what is left is silence. Hearing the silence after om is said to be an access point to one of the goals of yoga, which is to hear the unstruck sound.

NADA YOGA

In the *Hatha Yoga Pradipika*, one of the foremost yogic texts, it is said that the goal of yoga, enlightenment or samadhi, is to hear the unstruck sound, the sound beyond silence. This illustrates the journey from the external world to the more subtle experiences that yoga practices foster. But first we need to learn to hear the external sounds. We start by listening to the world outside, then we go in and see what we can hear in the internal world. When we start to practise deep listening, as part of a nada yoga practice, we notice how quickly we make meaning of everything. We hear a sound and the mind wants to categorise it. Instead, by trying to just listen to sounds without story or making meaning, we learn to drop things and move on. We train ourselves to listen more, be curious, stay very present, and not hold on to our feelings and beliefs. These are very powerful ways to start to work with forgiveness. Then as we turn our listening inwards, to the quieter, subtle parts of ourselves, we connect to that eternal Self. Part of that process is finding profound inner peace and strength, and the other part is feeling how we are always connected to everyone and everything. It is in this united, quieter place we can find the true inner strength to forgive.

Holding onto anger, resentment and grudges disturbs the energy flow within the body. By loosening our grip on negative emotions and practising forgiveness, we restore balance and harmony, allowing us to live with vitality and purpose.

DISTURBING THE CHEMISTRY: A SUMMARY

- Everything in existence, including our physical and emotional well-being, is governed by energy and vibration.
- Many ancient cultures have explored subtle anatomy, where the flow of energy within the body is seen as more significant than physical anatomy. It's all

about balance and flow.

- From a quantum perspective, all matter is vibration.
- Sound and frequencies can influence our well-being.
- Nada yoga focuses on hearing subtle internal sounds that go beyond the external world.

NADA YOGA – DEEP LISTENING

Nada yoga helps us learn to listen without judgement and pull in, so we can connect with that deep, internal part of the self. When we practise nada yoga, we notice how quickly we hear sounds, give them a label and make meaning of the external world. So, as we learn deeper listening, we try to hear things for what they are – vibration – and then eventually hear the internal sounds, which allows us to connect with who we are. It's like diving down into the oceanic depths of the soul.

EXERCISE

Sit down and make sure you're comfortable. Check that your jaw and face are relaxed and that your spine is straight without being stiff. As you close your eyes, listen to the sounds around you. Observe how quickly you label things. You might hear a sound and think it's a bird or a car. Instead of making meaning out of each sound, listen and move on to the next. Acknowledge every little sound, searching for the loudest and the quietest. This trains the brain to not just seek the loudest thoughts, which are often negative, but also quieter, connected ones. Over time, see how far you can hear sounds, then pull in and notice what you can hear close by. The next step is to turn inwards and listen to internal sounds. Can you hear your heart beating, your blood flowing? What else is there? Sit and listen to the more subtle, vast and deep parts of the ocean self.

MIND-BODY CONNECTION

The pathways between our thoughts and the physical body are intrinsically linked. Even when we are daydreaming, lost in thought or when our minds are racing, neurons get fired up and the physical body receives the chemicals and signals as though it's happening in real time. A 2021 study at University of California, San Francisco found that stuck, negative thoughts can lead to anger and stress, which can reduce our lifespan as it shortens our telomeres – the part of our DNA that protects our genetic data. Just like the energetic models suggest, we cannot think without impacting our physical form, and vice versa. Exercise and regular physical activity have been shown to increase neuroplasticity and mental flexibility, in addition to many other substantial benefits for the brain, including increasing blood flow, improving memory and reducing depression and anxiety.

There are many ways we can work with the mind and beyond the mind, outside in, to shift our thoughts and feelings. From using sound, eye movements and tapping to feeling sensations, laughing and crying. There are so many paths to forgiveness that don't require words, thinking, talking or giving anything up. Finding the right approach for us is where the fun begins.

BALANCED CHOICE

When it comes to understanding how to release pain from your past and create a brighter future, the first person who comes to mind is my dear friend Drakey. And he testifies to the importance of releasing things physically first.

I ask Drakey how he gets the kids working with forgiveness and what tools he uses in the Balanced Choice sessions. He tells me it's all about starting with the physical. The boys do a fitness session before diving into some breathwork together. Stretching out the neck is an important part of the exercise, with a focus on resetting the vagus nerve. Then they test their balance, which Drakey believes is crucial. It's all about getting grounded before they do the real work together. Then he finds they're ready to do some healing.

When they focus on forgiveness, he will ask them to define it, what it means to them. He leaves a lot of time and space for that, because every time these young people come in with an idea of what they think it is, they each have their own unique, powerful lens, and he's blown away by their perspectives. Laughter crackles through as he assures me they're always better than his, and that it is one of the many ways in which these kids transform him on a daily basis. He brings in quotes on forgiveness, and if they've brought something in, they read them too. They choose one together and agree that this is what forgiveness is going to represent for them that day. That's when the theatre comes in.

This involves role-play and theatre games. It might be a game like Octopus Tag, where you gather people as they get tagged, and they become an arm of the octopus, also helping to tag people. But as more people join the octopus, it gets harder to move. Drakey says: 'It basically starts off with just you, but we go through life and we gather all these things. And as soon as we gather more things that we're upset by and we're hurt by, we're unable to go in certain directions. Because we just can't even move anymore, it's like a weight on us. And so I always like to just have a bit of an edit about 'what can I put down?' So that game explores the idea that if we keep gathering stuff and keep gathering bad experiences, then we're almost unable to move anymore. And I'm all about, how do we bring freedom back, so we can move again? And freedom is in forgiveness.'

But it's the work at the end that he finds the most transformative. They explore past forgiveness, present forgiveness and future forgiveness.

The important part is being clear about what you need to forgive and making a commitment to it. Then, they mark that moment clearly by cutting a string, putting something around their arm, giving themselves a gift, writing something or getting a tattoo. It doesn't matter what it is as long as it honours that moment clearly. It says: 'I'm a clean canvas, I'm ready to step into the life I deserve.'

'I haven't been through what these kids have, and I'm very aware of my privilege,' says Drakey. 'And at the same time, life has provided me with plenty of challenges and still does daily. Every time I think I've sufficiently released all the pain there possibly can be left from a past betrayal, like one of those little Russian dolls, I find there's another layer inside.'

MOVEMENT AND THE MIND

Brad Stocks is a seasoned personal trainer with over twenty years of experience in the health and fitness industry. Motivated by a desire to support individuals on a deeper psychological level, he is currently completing a bachelor's degree in counselling and branching into the mental health field. I've been training with him for nearly ten years, and over that time, we've had endless conversations about movement, mindfulness and this mind-body loop. Brad says that he got into personal training as a way to help people feel better and alleviate their suffering: 'Because essentially, they're turning up and they're saying, "I'm not right and I want to change it, and you know, then I'll be happy. So we're going to work towards this goal, and then I'll be happy."'

He often saw people set physical goals, thinking that once they hit their target weight happiness would follow. But even after hitting that weight, they didn't feel any different. It was then he realised the issue was much deeper. People weren't unhappy because of their weight or appearance; they were unhappy at a deeper, emotional level.

This led him to study psychology, where he realised that the real reason people came to him was because they were struggling with something deeper. He says the importance of the mind-body connection cannot be underestimated, noting that movement can be a powerful way to practise mindfulness and release stored trauma. And he draws the connection between movement and mindfulness by explaining that when people engage in physical activities, whether it's weight training or playing a sport, they experience brief moments of presence. This presence, he says, mirrors the mindfulness found in meditation. It doesn't matter if it's lifting weights or hitting a tennis ball, any sport that requires focus will bring someone into the present moment. Movement forces people into the present moment: 'When you're doing a heavy back squat, it forces you to be present. You can't think about the future, you can't think about the past.'

He references the work of Bessel van der Kolk and his book *The Body Keeps the Score*, which discusses how trauma is stored in the body and can be released through movement. He explains that when people exercise, they move out of their amygdala into their prefrontal cortex, where they can think more clearly. He describes this process as a way to access deeper problem-solving abilities, highlighting how breathing and focusing on movement can allow someone to 'see things for how they really are', rather than through the lens of their anger and resentment

This is like the physical practice of yoga, or asana, where we are placing our body, mind, breath and attention in skilful and specific ways. You can't balance on one leg or your hands and be thinking about your narcissistic ex. You must be present, or you'll fall over. Moving your body mindfully shifts your perceptions.

SOMATIC THERAPY

There is a growing body of evidence on the mind-body connection and the potential for body-based therapies to support mental health, like the 2021 study led by Steven Davey. And research by Jennifer West and colleagues on treatment for post-traumatic stress disorder and chronic childhood abuse has revealed that traditional trauma treatments often fail but that body-based practices like trauma-informed yoga can be powerful complementary therapies to improve mental health and wellbeing. Brad describes it in this way:

> Somatic therapy has the essence of a lot of trauma therapy in that they start from the bottom up (the body) not top down (the mind, like CBT) – it ties

with polyvagal theory and is ultimately what a lot of us are doing by accident when we exercise. Polyvagal theory just describes how the evolutionary pathways of our autonomic nervous system influence our emotional and social behaviour in response to safety and danger, especially in the presence of others.

Some meditation practices also take this bottom-up approach, focusing on the body instead of just trying to concentrate on a mantra or the breath. In Vipassana meditation, rather than concentrating the mind on something, you focus on sensations in the physical body to notice how they are always changing. They come and go, just like our thoughts. Maybe they get more intense, dissipate and then another one arises. Meditating with this focus on what is happening in the body can be an excellent way to practise meditation, especially if you find other forms of meditation, where the focus is on something else, don't work for you.

EMDR

Eye movement desensitisation and reprocessing (EMDR) therapy is an empirically validated psychotherapy approach discovered by Francine Shapiro in the 1980s when she was a psychology student. She noticed there was a relationship between her eye movements and memory. This led her to research whether it had any impact on other people, and she found it did. It was particularly helpful with persistent upsetting memories. As we discussed, we know that painful memories may cause rumination, and interrupting the circuit, or processing those memories, can foster forgiveness.

EMDR does exactly that. It uses specific eye movements to help process painful memories in a safe, supportive space, so that we can let them go and forgive. Despite initial cynicism about its effectiveness, a huge body of research now shows it is highly beneficial, and in 2014 Shapiro reviewed all the evidence, including randomised studies and significant clinical reports. Her review confirmed the EMDR provides an efficient approach to address psychological and physiologic symptoms stemming from adverse life experiences. One study she reviewed, conducted at Kaiser Permanente, found 100% of single-trauma victims and 77% of multiple-trauma victims no longer had PTSD after six EMDR sessions. Another by the National Institute of Mental Health found it was more helpful than medication such as Prozac in many cases. Unlike CBT,

EMDR is considered gentler, as there is no extended time spent with the memories or detailed description of the events, and no homework, so it can be more accessible for some.

Psychologist Karen Asgill says, 'The process of diminishing the emotional intensity of a traumatic memory can be a profound one for an individual. The process of EMDR offers the opportunity for all parts of the brain to come together and process what has primarily been stored in the body and the emotional (limbic) system, which is what is activated when similar sensory experiences are encountered. Bilateral stimulation allows the two hemispheres of the brain to talk to each other, so that disturbing memories become more objective. From the place of objectivity, it becomes more possible (although not guaranteed) that forgiveness can take place. I often find that there is a "softening" and a less defensive place that clients can now go which is very helpful to interpersonal relationships and feelings.'

EFT

Emotional freedom technique (EFT) is an evidence-based therapeutic method which involves tapping the

12 meridian points on the body. Over 100 studies demonstrate its efficacy, including a 2019 study by Donna Bach. The research shows it improves both mental and physical well-being, and the beauty lies in its simplicity and accessibility. You don't have to get it one hundred per cent accurate. You are using your fingers for a few moments to tap on one of the twelve meridian points, which are thought to regulate our system in different ways.

Vicki Smart, founder of Mission Yoga & Therapeutics, tells me that EFT is powerful, particularly when it comes to forgiveness and strong emotions. It creates a buffer between you and the mind reacting to big emotions. She says that tapping is self-care; we are lovingly touching ourselves. To activate the parasympathetic nervous system, she tells me to stimulate one particular kidney point, K27, which can get us out of fight-or-flight. It is calming, which helps the vagus nerve access the parasympathetic nervous system.

To do it, she suggests gentle tapping under the collar bones with the finger pads, roughly in the middle. But don't stress too much about the exact spot. If it's in the general area, you are stimulating and bringing awareness to the right place energetically. This is the beauty of tapping. You can't really get it wrong. I find myself doing it frequently when

I'm wired, dysregulated or winding down to go to bed.

As a bonus, Vicki also suggests lying on your tummy on a rolled-up blanket directly under the belly, and taking slow, deep breaths. The vagal nerve also runs through the belly and breath is key here. She says: 'Remember, with everything we have access to, with all the research and tools we have, that deep breaths are still the number one technique to access a calm state of being.'

TEARS

Part of the definition and process of forgiveness is releasing. And a very powerful and scientifically proven way to do that is by having a cry. We are the only animal that cries as an emotional response. Tears help release and reset because the hormones found in emotional tears are thought to be emitted to help us regulate and bring us back into balance. A 2014 study found that crying may have many physiological effects that set us up well for forgiveness; they may decrease aggression, stress and cortisol in the body, while increasing feel-good chemicals, trust, empathy and bonding between people. Their onset might engage the sympathetic nervous system, but the release that occurs takes us into the parasympathetic nervous state, where we are better placed to start the process of letting go and forgiving.

GETTING UNSTUCK – BREAKING THE CIRCUIT

In some cases, interrupting the rumination and stress response cycle may be the easiest way to work with forgiveness without having to process what has happened at a psychological level. Many ancient practices speak to this concept and provide practical ways to break the circuit.

In the *Yoga Sutras*, Patanjali talks about the mind getting stuck on a loop, thoughts whirling, like a needle glitching on an old record. Yoga and mindfulness practices are designed to interrupt the loop and free the mind from this tendency. In TCM, they also recognise that energy gets stuck in certain parts of the body and mind, so acupuncture interrupts that circuit to release the trapped 'chi' or energy.

When my girlfriend first discovered her husband's affair, the rumination was relentless, and no matter what she did to distract herself, her mind kept circling back obsessively to the betrayal. To break the cycle, she kept a red 'stop!' sign in her pocket at all times. She would pull it out, hold it in her hands, look at it, and consciously say 'stop!' That sign was the beginning of starting again, of training her brain to interrupt the circuit. It helped to pull her out of the whirlpool back into the present moment where she needed to be if she had any hope of looking to the future.

THE VAGUS NERVE

One of the best ways to break the circuit and get out of the fight-or-flight state is to trigger the parasympathetic state, and our mighty hero, the vagus nerve, is the very guy for the job. Carrying a whopping 75 per cent of all parasympathetic nerve fibres in the body, the vagus nerve is the primary component of the cool, calm and collected parasympathetic nervous system. It has a direct relationship with emotional regulation, social connectedness, and our capacity to forgive.

In one landmark study in 2010, Barbara Fredrickson and Bethany Kok found that vagal tone is directly linked to social and psychological well-being. Vagal tone refers to how well the vagal nerve is functioning. The study showed there was an upward spiral, which created a feedback loop. Genuine moments of social connectedness between people triggered the parasympathetic nervous system and toned the vagus nerve, creating positive feedback and emotions, leading to further expansion of social networks, which triggers the parasympathetic state, and on the loop goes. People with higher vagal tone had better overall heart health, lower levels of inflammation. They also had stronger social bonds and exhibited better emotional regulation which makes forgiveness way more accessible.

In 2013 further research by Fredrickson and Kok found that practising loving kindness meditation with yourself and others is the key to turbo-charging this upward spiral of vagal tone, heightening parasympathetic nervous system activity. A loving kindness meditation involves thinking about yourself, and specific people, and sending goodwill, kindness and love. The key to fostering the upward spiral of vagal tone is sending loving kindness not just to the ones we love, which can be relatively easy, but to enemies, and those we hold a grudge towards. Loving kindness meditation is also a very powerful circuit breaker when stuck in feelings of rage, as it consciously changes the channel to a different frequency, from anger to benevolence. It shifts us back into our humanity and reconnects us with our compassion.

The beauty of all this is that we can work with the vagus nerve in very practical ways, such as through simple breath practices, meditation and taking regular breaks throughout the day. Exercise, including endurance and interval training, as well as stretching and gentle massage, particularly of the neck, shoulders and feet, are also effective. Reflexology, short-term exposure to cold temperatures like cold plunges or ending showers with cold water, and fostering feelings of awe through music, nature or meaningful experiences can further stimulate the vagus nerve. Even tapping techniques offer an accessible way to support its function. And in doing these exercises, without even consciously having to process the thoughts and feelings associated, we are giving ourselves the best possible chance of forgiving.

MINDFULNESS FOR THE AMYGDALA

Though it has ancient roots, the modern understanding of mindfulness – the process of paying attention to the present moment, on purpose, free from judgement – was coined by Jon Kabat-Zinn. Jennifer R. Wolkin, PhD, neuropsychologist brings together a body of research in her article on how the brain changes with mindfulness. Mindfulness has been shown to help decrease the size of the fight-or-flight captain, the amygdala, and increase the density of the prefrontal cortex, which is the part of the brain responsible for 'keeping us calm and carrying on', when it comes to our emotions. It also creates a stronger connectivity between the reactive amygdala and the rational, relaxed prefrontal cortex, which means less reactivity. And increased grey matter changes were noted in the anterior cingulate cortex, which is behind the brain's frontal lobe. It has been associated with self-regulation and allows for more cognitive flexibility. Less reactivity, better regulation and greater cognitive flexibility all mean a greater capacity to forgive.

LAUGHTER

The Mayo Clinic highlights the therapeutic benefits of laughter, showcasing its ability to alleviate tension, increase feel-good chemicals to the brain like endorphins, and lower the stress response and therefore the heart rate and blood pressure. It can make it easier to cope with difficult situations and connect to people, reduce anxiety and depression, and improve self-esteem. This may explain why so many people who manage to forgive the unforgivable, like Simi surviving her traumatic childhood and Matt Backer getting through his years of bullying, credit laughter as being such a critical factor.

BREATH

Brooke Elliston's journey into breathwork began unexpectedly while working as a banking litigation lawyer. After four and a half years, she developed troubling symptoms like numbness, full-body rashes and a choking sensation. When her legs gave way at work, a trip to the emergency room revealed a surprising diagnosis: chronic hyperventilation. This wake-up call revealed the profound connection between our breath, body and mind. Brooke realised that hyperventilation wasn't just a symptom of stress but a root cause.

Her healing began when she turned to pranayama, the yogic science of breath finesse and suspension. Through breath holds, she accessed deep mental calm that willpower alone couldn't reach. In yoga, pranayama precedes meditation because it stills the mind by slowing and eventually suspending the breath. Scientifically, the effects are simple but powerful. Brooke says: 'Breath holds increase carbon dioxide levels, triggering relaxation, expanding your airways and enhancing oxygen delivery to the heart and brain through the Bohr effect. Breathwork acts as a powerful circuit breaker, leading from anxiety to calm and creating the ideal internal space for healing and forgiveness.'

PSYCHOLOGY

From a psychological perspective, there are varying ideas about what forgiveness really entails. Research conducted at Ludwig-Maximilians-University of Munich found that there are two significant dimensions: decisional and emotional forgiveness. Though it may be an important first step to decide to forgive, to truly do so, emotional forgiveness replaces negative thoughts towards the transgressor with positive ones, such as love or empathy. Decisional forgiveness is the cognitive letting go of resentment and bitterness. However, it's not the end of emotional pain. Emotional forgiveness is often required for people to fully move on.

The process of forgiveness is voluntary; it requires a person to be receptive. There were many people I approached for this book, people I admire and love, who didn't want to take part. Some of them just said, 'Look, I'm not there yet. It may appear I have forgiven, but I haven't really.' Forgiveness is not something you can force. Patience is key, and having the deepest compassion for yourself wherever you are is the most important thing.

Therapy may cultivate this readiness and foster acceptance, empathy, perspective and a focus on the benefits rather than the negative impacts of the offence. Positive psychology suggests exercises such as rewriting the story of what happened in a journal and taking a different perspective as a way of working through anger and promoting healing. Similarly, the *Yoga Sutras* advise that when we experience disturbing thoughts, we should think of the opposite, flip thoughts upside down and see things from a completely different perspective. Or as the Stoic Epictetus says, 'What assistance can we find in the fight against habit? Try the opposite!'

CBT

Cognitive behavioural therapy (CBT) is a psychological treatment that has been demonstrated to be beneficial in addressing both cognitive and emotional aspects of forgiveness. Rather than focusing on the past, CBT focuses on present thinking patterns, learned behaviours and fostering better ways to cope with problems. The idea is to recognise that distorted thinking patterns like anger may be creating cycles of bitterness and suffering. CBT addresses these distortions by helping individuals directly face their fears instead of avoiding them. This often incorporates emotional forgiveness, where negative thoughts are replaced with more positive, rational, compassionate ones. As the American Psychological Association says, it's a collaborative process, empowering individuals to become their own therapists and to move forward by changing unhelpful ways of thinking. Through this, people can let go of anger and resentment, fostering both decisional and emotional forgiveness.

MIND-BODY CONNECTION: A SUMMARY

- The mind-body connection shows we can use many ways to break the circuit – physical, mental or energetic.
- We can help down regulation via breath, the vagus nerve, compassion and mindfulness practices.
- Laughter and tears help us release.
- Techniques like breathwork and mindfulness break emotional pain cycles.
- Decisional forgiveness is letting go of resentment; emotional forgiveness replaces negative thoughts with empathy.
- Forgiveness is a voluntary process that can't be forced.
- Psychology provides different therapies to work through forgiveness, like CBT, EMDR, EFT and positive psychology.

BREATH HOLDS

There are many ways to break the circuit of fight-or-flight or rumination and get the mental calm and space required for forgiveness. As Brooke suggested, one way is to practice breath holds. When done carefully, they can be very powerful. But they are not for everyone, so if the practise below creates any tension or stress, pause for shorter periods, or don't do the holds at all, just practise inhaling and exhaling slowly.

EXERCISE

Inhale gently through the nose. Exhale effortlessly, and at the bottom of the exhale, pinch your nose and hold your breath for a few seconds. *(Note: Without pinching, air may still flow in and out.)* Resume normal breathing for 2-3 breaths. Inhale again and exhale gently. This time, hold your breath for 3-5 seconds. Repeat this cycle for 2-3 minutes, practising once per hour or as needed throughout the day.

FORGIVE YOURSELF FIRST

Drakey's program Balanced Choice was first implemented in Dondale, the main youth detention facility in the Northern Territory, which was still part of the adult prison at that time. Even though the program was up and running, Drakey was not well. While working in Tennant Creek, he got himself into a dark, unhealthy place, struggling with alcoholism and the collateral damage it leaves in its wake. He would go into Dondale, run the program, and listen to the boys talk about all sorts of things. But every time they spoke about forgiveness, he found himself emotional and teary, and he realised how unwell he really was.

It was those young men who helped him recover. They pointed him to his own forgiveness. The program was a huge success. The kids loved it, and they loved him, long before he even liked himself. Each time he showed up, they were so excited and engaged and he was dumbfounded by how and why they loved him. It was through this love, and his lack of self-love, that he realised he needed to stop, take a look inside and face the things he was ashamed and scared of: the things he carried from his past, the things in his closet, the mistakes he'd made, the things that haunted him, the parts of himself he wasn't proud of. It was only through acknowledging them, and then putting those things down, that he realised he could then share those stories with others. It was his self-forgiveness that enabled him to share his journey, giving those kids permission to find their own voice for their healing, and empowering them to heal themselves too. As he says, 'your stories may well be the key that unlocks the stories, and healing, in others'.

He sees that cycle again and again in Balanced Choice as staff come on board and go through their own process of self-forgiveness and self-love. There's not much data on the rate of young people returning to prison in Australia, and it's complicated at best. But one of the factors contributing to re-offending seems to be age. The older you get, the harder it is to avoid re-offending. It's easier to intervene earlier and give young people the tools and opportunity to change their lives and make better choices. Balanced Choice has now transformed the lives of over five thousand young people and their families, and the ripple-on effect is immeasurable. Drakey firmly believes the secret to moving towards a life you really want is by looking in the mirror. 'You have to be able to look at yourself, forgive yourself for everything, and love yourself more.'

When you are working with Indigenous cultural understanding, once you acknowledge and understand the past and present suffering that you may have contributed to, a critical step is forgiving yourself. Carla Rogers from Evolve says when guilt gets in the way of being an ally, self-forgiveness is key:

> So as an ally, and as part of forgiveness, it's being prepared to seek feedback on, and look at the impact of, your actions. Being open to feedback on that impact. And then the big part of that is forgiving yourself, being kind to yourself if you have had unintended consequences. And then it's learning from it and course correcting. It's a lifelong journey, like washing the dishes. You just keep getting up every day and doing it.

RECOVERY

I met Osher Günsberg almost two decades ago. The beauty of knowing people over long periods of time is that you get to witness how they grow and change. The Osher I met was dating a friend of mine, working on *Australian Idol* and living his best Bondi bachelor life. But the Osher I now know is a highly intelligent, curious, compassionate, sober dad of two. In the same way, I am not the same Rachael he met back then. He speaks openly about his mental health and addiction challenges and the importance of forgiving himself:

> One of the twelve steps that I took when I first got sober was to go through all of the awful things I'd done to myself and others. An exercise book filled with a searching and fearless inventory of every awful thing that I'd ever done ... to look at all of it in one giant pile of horribleness was overwhelming. But then I told my sponsor every single one of those things. It was brutal, and when we were done, I was an empty shell. That's when he told me something which helped me move forward on that day, and has helped me every day of the

fourteen and a bit years since then: 'I've got good news for you, pal, you get to live the rest of your life not being that guy anymore.'

Accepting and acknowledging the behaviour and the choices that I made gives me something to do with the energy which shows up when I remember moments of regret. Rather than those memories kicking off a self-sustaining loop of self-flagellation, I am now able to redirect that energy into action. I do not have access to a time machine. I cannot change the choices I made, but I can make better choices. So instead of wallowing in self-destruction, or getting caught in 'coulda, shoulda, woulda' thinking, I get to make choices which are more aligned with how I want to live my life now. Because I get to live my life not being that guy anymore.

GUILT VS SHAME

We often speak of these two negative emotions, guilt and shame, in the same way, but researchers say they are very different. In an interview with the American Psychological Association, June Tangney, a professor at George Mason

University and author of *Shame and Guilt*, summarises it in this way: 'Well, people feel shame and guilt for all manner of failures and transgressions, but the difference is when people feel shame, they feel badly about themselves; when people feel guilt, they feel badly about a specific behaviour.'

Tangney says that guilt can be useful in promoting a group's well-being, as people try to do the right thing by one another to stay connected to their community. Feelings of guilt can be then viewed as useful from an evolutionary perspective, because when we act in a way that harms others and feel bad about how we behaved, we may then work to repair the damage we caused. Guilt has also been associated with empathy, which builds connections to others.

Shame, on the other hand, tends to turn the negative thoughts on ourselves, diminishing our sense of self. This does the opposite of what evolution intended, and rather than leading to socially constructive behaviours, shame can be painful and debilitating and lead to a negative cycle.

When we behave in a way that causes harm, guilt is constructive because we observe our action or behaviour and work to remedy and change it. Shame, on the other hand, is when we turn the spotlight on our sense of self, seeing ourselves as imperfect and bad, rather than the action itself. Guilt can create a connection when we take positive action. Shame is destructive and creates self-loathing and disconnection.

FAILURE AS AN ELITE ATHLETE

Australian surfing legend Sally Fitzgibbons has had a lifelong love for sport and the ocean. In 2007, she claimed gold in the 800m and 1500m track events at the Australian Youth Olympic Festival, racing on the same track where Freeman once warmed up. Sally's surfing career is a testament to her grit, determination and never-give-up attitude. In addition to her decorated athletic career, Sally became an Olympian at Tokyo 2021, where she finished fifth in surfing's Olympic debut, and is a member of the International Olympic Committee, working to ensure future success for the Games. I talk to her while she is in Portugal doing what she loves – surfing in a comp. She says embracing imperfection and failure is key:

> 'It wasn't good enough, I'm not good enough, what are people going to think of me, I've let my team

> down' … you go through all these thoughts, and after an enormous amount of energy, you finally arrive at a place of forgiveness to move forward and try again. If all that energy spent on emotional outbursts about failure could be channelled back into the process, your growth rate and emotional stability would trend up at a faster rate … It's about not desiring more than the opportunity to just do your process, which leads to high performance.
>
> Forgiveness might just be the bungee jump cable in it all, the only lifeline as you jump off the platform into the unknown of the performance. The ability to forgive yourself for not being perfect is growth in itself. It can be an opportunity for others around you to find it in themselves too.

In the high-stakes world of elite sport, where failure is inevitable, she says, 'forgiveness may just be one of our most valuable human qualities in order to have a sustainable existence'. And she reminds us: 'Don't you love that the main saying around practice is "practice makes perfect"? In this case, we can take the opportunity to rephrase it into "practice comes with forgiveness".'

Sally reminds us that in the pursuit of excellence, learning to forgive yourself for not being perfect is just as vital as the desire to succeed.

REGRET

The *American Heritage Dictionary* defines regret as; to feel sorry, disappointed, distressed, or remorseful, to remember with a feeling of loss or sorrow, to mourn. It comes from the Middle English 'regretten', to lament, and the Old French 'regrater', to weep. The *Merriam-Webster Dictionary* defines it as sorrow aroused by circumstances beyond one's control or power to repair and can also be understood as an expression of distressing emotion.

For those of you who have heard iconic French singer Edith Piaf's infamous song 'Non, je ne regrette rien', you'd be hard-pressed not to feel moved and optimistic. Piaf's uplifting anthem seems a cruel contrast to her tragic life, steeped in misfortune from her birth, and yet her message is loud and clear: 'No, I do not regret anything.' Born on the streets of Paris in 1915, abandoned by her mother, she was brought up by prostitutes in the brothel her grandmother ran. She suffered from ill-health from an early age, even being blinded for four years in her infancy due to meningitis. At just 17, she gave birth to a daughter of her own, who died at two of meningitis, and the great love of her life boxer Marcel Cerdan was killed in a plane crash on his way to see her. So many things beyond our power to control or repair can create immense frustration and suffering. But they can also be overcome, and in the case of so many artists like Piaf, pain can be transformed through storytelling into art, sharing the human experience with people across the world, and lasting a lifetime.

Regret is viewed by many psychologists as an evolutionary advantage for a species to learn from previous mistakes and avoid them in the future. When we don't learn and get stuck in a cycle of self-flagellation, we suffer.

Dealing with regret is difficult because of other negative emotions connected to it: remorse, sorrow and helplessness. According to research by Colleen Saffrey and colleagues, 'individuals who ruminate on their regrets are more likely to report reduced life satisfaction and to experience difficulty coping with negative life events'. And a study at Concordia University found regret has many negative mental and physical effects, including throwing off the balance of hormones and immune systems.

In a study by Shai Davidai and Thomas Gilovich, action-related regrets, although painful, seem to spur people to learn from their mistakes and move on. But regret related to inaction – the things undone, the opportunities lost – is harder to fix. This kind of regret is more likely to lead to depression, anxiety, a sense of 'stuckness' and a feeling of longing over not knowing what could have been.

The Stoics viewed regret as a learning opportunity. Rather than getting consumed by it, they suggested we reflect on our past with curiosity and a willingness to learn. Understanding our missteps can provide insights that inform future decisions, turning past errors into valuable lessons. They had three key rules to overcome regret:

1. Focus on what you can control.
2. Embrace everything that happens to you in life ('amor fati') as it has a meaning, even if you can't see it.
3. Prepare for the future.

As we saw earlier, Epictetus said, we should forgive others, as well as ourselves, over and over and over again. Then try to do better next time.

WHAT HAPPENS WHEN WE LET GO OF REGRET

Psychoanalyst Erik Erikson argues that as we get older, we move to a stage of either 'ego integrity' or 'despair'. If we can look back on our life satisfied, with a sense of wisdom, accomplishment, wholeness, acceptance and fulfilment, we are in ego integrity. If we reflect on it with shame, regret, bitterness and disdain, we feel despair. Research by Holger Busch and colleagues illustrated that the ultimate fear – death anxiety – is eased with ego integrity and heightened with despair. In other words, if we are accepting and content towards the end of our life we will have less fear about our mortality.

If we want to approach our final days, weeks, months of this life with more peace and less fear, we must work with regret. The more we can forgive ourselves for all the things we did, or didn't do, the healthier and happier we will be for the time we have left in this precious life.

FORGIVE YOURSELF FIRST: A SUMMARY

- Self-forgiveness is the first step towards healing.
- In addiction recovery, self-forgiveness is crucial for moving forward.
- Guilt focuses on the behaviour and leads to constructive change, while shame internalises negativity and can be destructive.
- Forgive yourself daily, like washing the dishes.
- Elite athletes must accept failure as part of growth.
- Regret is a natural emotion, but regret over missed opportunities is harder to overcome than regret from mistakes.
- Focus on what you can control, accept life as it unfolds (amor fati), and prepare for the future.
- Holding onto regret leads to despair, while acceptance fosters wisdom and reduces anxiety.

MINDFULNESS AND SELF-FORGIVENESS

Mindfulness practices play a positive role in self-forgiveness and forgiveness. According to a review of research on mindfulness and forgiveness by psychologist and research scientist Dr Grace Bullock, students with higher mindfulness scores were more willing to consider another person's perspective, which was associated with a greater likelihood to forgive.

EXERCISE

Find a comfortable seat. Shift your awareness to the body. Notice how you feel. Now shift your awareness to your breath. Don't change it. Just let it move in its natural rhythm. Watch it moving in and out. Focus on the exhale. This will help slow the breath down and harness your awareness. Scan the body for any sensations. As thoughts arise, simply give them a label without going into meaning or story, such as 'regret', 'anger', 'hatred' or 'sadness'. This allows us to get a bit of distance from the emotion, becoming an observer instead. Stay like this for a few minutes if you can. When you finish, notice how you feel.

IMPERFECTION

We all know there are two types of LEGO kids, just as there are two types of IKEA adults: those who buy the sets and adhere to the instructions, keeping each one on display or in a sealed plastic bag, and those who have a giant bag of LEGO and prefer to creatively freestyle and pull apart at whim. Emmet's journey in the LEGO film was to let go of his attachment to the perfect world he lived in and embrace all the possibilities and inventiveness of an instruction-free zone. But the deal with innovation is we have to welcome imperfection.

IT ALL STARTED WITH A BANG

The leading explanation for how the universe began is the Big Bang theory. As the name suggests, it is believed that our existence began not in a neat, ordered package but as an almighty, messy blast. Around 13.7 billion years ago, everything was concentrated in a tiny, singular, very hot point. Suddenly, there was an explosion and the universe expanded faster than the speed of light. Our very existence comes from a place of chaos. To be alive is a messy business, and no matter how hard we try, we can't control it.

PERFECTIONISM

Perfectionism is on the rise and it's affecting young people in detrimental ways. According to the World Health Organization, serious mental illness is affecting a record number of young people, and this upward trend appears to be continuing. Research by Thomas Curren and Andrew P Hill suggests that the increase in perfectionism may be one of the most important dimensions contributing to the rising mental health crisis we are witnessing. We must learn to embrace the messiness and imperfection of life if we wish to lessen our suffering in this lifetime. This involves accepting all the parts of ourselves – the good, the bad and the ugly.

The more we do this, the more we can move towards a state of self-acceptance and make the changes we need to. None of us are perfect. There's a Darth Vader in all of us. Recognising how flawed we are allows us to understand that other people are flawed too. Burying negative feelings, like hatred or shame, about ourselves and others serves no one.

VIRABHADRA

One of my favourite yogic myths is the story of Virabhadra, a great warrior mentioned in many Hindu texts. There are many versions of the story, but at the heart of the myth lies Shiva. He was a young, charismatic deity who meditated a lot. He met a gentle, loving princess named Sati and they fell in love. Sati's dad, Daksha, didn't like Shiva, who was known to have an epic temper, hang out with ghosts in graveyards, sport dreadlocks and wear a tiger skin. What's more, he was not a prince. Despite her dad's protests, Sati dug her heels in and married Shiva. Daksha threw a big party later and invited everyone except Sati and Shiva. Sati arrived at the party to confront her dad and protested (though some stories say she meditated) until she self-immolated. Shiva was furious, so he pulled out one of his dreadlocks, threw it on the ground and created a fierce warrior called Virabhadra to avenge her death. Virabhadra broke through the ground, brandishing his sword, raced to the party and chopped Daksha's head off. After discovering what Virabhadra had done, Shiva tried to find Daksha's head, but, unable to locate it, he found an excellent goat's head to replace it.

In this myth, Shiva represents our 'higher selves', the 'good' in us. Daksha represents our ego – our righteousness, judgements and fixed sense of the world. But even Shiva gets it wrong. The good in us can make mistakes. The good in us can have a little Virabhadra. We all make mistakes. And we can always make amends, however imperfect they are.

MISSING THE MARK

Rabbi Ninio also says Judaism recognises that everyone makes mistakes. The Hebrew word for sin is 'Chet', which is an archery term used when you aim for the bullseye but miss the mark. Humans strive to do good but like an archer, we're human and we miscue. We blunder all the time. The biblical stories are powerful in communicating this. Even Moses, who is considered to be the greatest prophet of all in Judaism, messes up all the time. We're flawed, and it's okay. As long as we recognise when we've done wrong, we correct our path and make a different choice the next time.

LEADERSHIP

After 25 years as a coach, facilitator and business owner, Duncan Young realised that one of the biggest challenges for leaders was managing the multiple and often conflicting needs of their stakeholders. He says, 'Depending on where the leader is situated within the organisational structure or hierarchy, their stakeholders are many and varied. Each stakeholder group will have its own priorities and pressures and within each group, there will be an array of individual wants, needs and ambitions.' Balancing fairness across different groups while staying focused on a long-term vision is not just an organisational challenge but a universal one. In this context, forgiveness is crucial. He says:

> I think leaders can forgive themselves for not having all the answers (if any). The complexity of the challenges we're all facing is so rapidly expanding, its often impossible to identify the 'right' thing to do. Tomorrow's problem will not be solved by today's thinking. For many leaders this is distressing. Two of the common traits of high-performing individuals are perfectionism and control. When there's no space for these, it can create a dissonance that results in the leader blaming themself for not being able to figure it out – or they project their distress onto others; either their team or other stakeholder groups.

Duncan says leaders must forgive themselves for not having all the answers, embrace imperfection, and stop blaming others for problems with complex origins. In this sense, forgiveness is about unburdening themselves from the responsibility of solving every problem and accepting the limitations of leadership.

YOU ARE MORE THAN THE WORST THING YOU'VE DONE

Drakey believes we should see people for their goodness, not their mistakes. In his work with young people in detention, he says it's not his job to find the worst in people. He's not the police. They've already got to wrestle with those things and they're normally front of mind for them. Instead, he directs people towards the best in themselves. And it's easier to do that for others when someone has done it for you.

Over the years, he has watched countless lives transformed with this mindset. He recently saw a kid he had worked with for many years and the young man said to him, 'You know, I haven't been back to prison for eight years.' He had also become a young dad. Drakey reflected that sometimes you need someone else to see your goodness, to show you that the shame that keeps being presented to you is not the whole story, and it's time to forgive yourself. This young man said the secret to being able to forgive himself was his kid. Drakey sees this transition to becoming a dad as one of the three main ways he witnesses young people forgiving themselves and making a real change in their lives. He says:

> I always say there's three windows where I see change in young people, when they do the work and find forgiveness for themselves. One is when they become a parent. The second is when one of their grandparents, or someone in their family, is quite sick. They don't want to be remembered as the kid that always caused the problems and was always getting locked up, so they just seem to turn things around. And the last one, as sad as it is, is kids just before they're about to turn eighteen. They do a fair bit of internal work on themselves, so they don't end up in the 'big house', the prison. They're the three things that I've witnessed, that make them really lean into forgiveness and transform their lives.

LETTING YOUNG PEOPLE MAKE MISTAKES

Daisy Turnbull, educator and author of *50 Questions to Ask Your Teens*, believes that teenagers today are engaging in the same behaviours as those of us who went before them, but now, it's all happening online and it lasts forever. They are going to parties, making poor decisions, having fights with their parents and wearing questionable outfits ... but the difference is that these moments are now captured and shared digitally. Even though they might delete these images from their profiles, we know they never truly disappear.

Teenagers are going to do what teenagers do, and society needs to decide whether to hold them accountable for these actions for the rest of their lives. Daisy compares this to the Amish tradition of Rumspringa, where young people are given the freedom to explore and make mistakes before returning to their community. It's not that we let teenagers act without any consequences. Rather, they should be able to move beyond the minor mistakes of their youth, just like we all did.

THE COMPLEXITY OF CANCEL CULTURE

Cancel culture is a phenomenon of our times, and like all things, it is a two-sided coin. On the one hand, we see more accountability, which shows we are evolving and setting boundaries. It can take down the rich and powerful in cases where the justice system has failed to do so, and it has been useful in addressing social injustices. A Canadian study led by Marissa Traversa suggests cancel culture may be effective in immediate harm-reduction for the harmed group, creating feelings of collective validation and a stronger intention to work for change.

On the flip side, a recent study by Linda Jonsson at Södertörn University, Stockholm also looked at the harm it may be causing to journalists and free speech as they become increasingly wary of what they say and censor themselves to stay safe. Censorship of our news is a high price to pay, but it's understandable when young journalists are punished for something someone perceives as offensive. This will ultimately limit the free flow of information and not give us all the perspectives in a complex world, especially if we silence every controversial opinion.

What would the world be like if no one could make mistakes? Accountability is important and cancel culture is also known as consequence culture. But what is the consequence? It doesn't open the door for understanding and conversation. It literally slams that door shut. It's not fostering constructive dialogue or healing. It doesn't provide space to be accountable and change, and as people are ostracised, the divide widens. People become more polarised. In *Mediations*, Marcus Aurelius writes:

> Whenever you take offense at someone's wrongdoing, immediately turn to your own similar failings, such as seeing money as good, or pleasure, or a little fame – whatever form it takes. By thinking on this, you'll quickly forget your anger, considering also what compels them – for what else could they do? Or, if you are able, remove their compulsion.

DON'T CRY OVER SPILT MILK

Most of us have heard the expression 'don't cry over spilt milk' used in the context of telling someone to wipe away their tears, get over it and move on. It's true to a point, but it's not that simple and shouldn't be received as a message to deny your feelings or dismiss your experience. Yes, when you spill a carton of milk, you're never going to be able to get the liquid back into the container. And if you do – by mopping and squeezing – it's not going to be the same. I certainly wouldn't be drinking it. We've all spilt milk before literally or metaphorically, and we've all had someone knock our drink over intentionally or unconsciously. But spilt drinks are the price we pay, the risk we take, if we are lucky enough to have our cup full in the first place. This is the nature of this very imperfect life. Our cup is full because we are alive. Sometimes we spill it and make a mess, sometimes we don't. The point is, we must learn to be okay with the chaos of life, with our cups full, or a sticky, wet floor. And we must have enough faith in ourselves to know we can always clean the mess up and fill our cup back up again. We can do it so many ways as we've discovered through our previous chapters. We can make art, practise mindfulness, do some breath holds, reset the vagus nerve, or go for a mindful walk.

As we will see in the next chapter, life is short. Tomorrow is promised to no one. So, raise your (empty or full) glass to this crazy, imperfect ride. Crack out that LEGO, or IKEA set, throw out your instructions, and embrace all the possibilities of what you can create. (Okay, maybe keep the IKEA instructions, just in case ...)

IMPERFECTION: A SUMMARY

- Embrace imperfection as a part of life and creativity.
- Life begins from chaos, not order. It's messy, and so are we.
- Perfectionism is on the rise. Accepting our imperfections is key to reducing suffering and fostering self-acceptance.
- Self-acceptance comes from acknowledging our flaws and strengths.
- Mistakes are a part of being human. The goal is to recognise when we miss the mark and correct our path.
- Leaders must accept they cannot please everyone and that making tough decisions comes with imperfection.
- When offended by others' mistakes, reflect on your own failings. It helps dissolve anger and foster empathy.
- You are more than your worst mistake.
- Young people should be allowed to make mistakes and learn from them.
- While cancel culture can hold people accountable, it often lacks space for understanding and growth.
- Don't cry over spilt milk, life is messy, but we can always clean it up or fill up our own cup.

BREATH WITH SOUND

Canadian yoga and breathwork teacher Sarah Routhier has been working with the human body since 2009. Starting as a sports and therapeutics registered massage therapist and yoga teacher, she now incorporates sound, bhakti and breathwork in classes, workshops, retreats and teacher trainings.

Her simple two-minute breath with sound practice is a great entry point for those wanting to work with sound vibration and tapping, or for those who need a regular circuit breaker they can come back to time and time again. I love it because it's very accessible, and I feel the calming effects every time I do it.

EXERCISE

With your mouth closed and eyes soft or closed, take a slow and intentional breath into the sides of your ribs. As you exhale, you are invited to keep your mouth closed and hum. You could simply do this or add on by tapping your sternum/chest bone gently with your fingers. Do this 5–10 times or play your favourite two-minute song.

MEMENTO MORI

'Memento mori,' which means 'remember you must die' in Latin, is a philosophical practice that emphasises the importance of mortality in guiding how we live our lives. Stoic thinkers like Seneca and Marcus Aurelius highlighted the necessity of keeping death at the forefront of our minds to foster a deeper appreciation for the present, encouraging us to live meaningfully and forgive and let go of the past and what we cannot control.

In his letters, Seneca wrote a lot about remembering our mortality and living each day as though it were our last: 'Let us compose our thoughts as if we've reached the end. Let us postpone nothing. Let's settle our accounts with life every day.'

Epictetus told his students to always remember the people they love are mortal: 'If you are kissing your child or wife, say that it is a human being whom you are kissing, for when the wife or child dies, you will not be disturbed.'

The idea is to remember we are going to die so we can live our lives more fully. As Marcus Aureliu wrote, 'Think of yourself as dead. You have lived your life. Now, take what's left and live it properly.'

Bhutanese traditions and Buddhist teachings echo this sentiment, promoting daily contemplation of death as a means to cultivate compassion, mindfulness and a richer, more fulfilling life. Maranasati meditation, for example, is a series of Buddhist mindfulness practices that remind us of our death.

Author Eric Weiner, who researched and wrote a book on happiness, *The Geography of Bliss: One Grump's Search for the Happiest Places in the World*, says that Bhutan is consistently ranked as one of the happiest places in the world, and he believes it may be connected to death awareness. Weiner believes the key to their happiness is by remembering their death, five times a day. They do practise ahimsa – non-violence – like many other nations, and they focus on building a healthy and fulfilling life for their citizens, but the most different, and perhaps interesting aspect of their culture, is that they contemplate death daily.

Unlike much of western culture, the Bhutanese don't hide death. Much of the art and Buddhist iconography has death as its themes and imagery. When someone dies there is a 49-day mourning period. It does make some sense to think about death so much. One of the studies Weiner looked at, showed 'death is a psychologically threatening fact, but when people contemplate it, apparently the automatic system begins to search for happy thoughts'. By remembering that we are all dying, we stop sweating the small stuff, realise that nothing is permanent, focus on the present and enjoy our lives. Or as Steve Jobs said: 'Remembering that I'll be dead soon is the most important tool I've ever encountered to help me make the big choices in life. Because almost everything – all external expectations, all pride, all fear of embarrassment or failure – these things just fall away in the face of death, leaving only what is truly important.'

CARPE DIEM

I have an app on my phone called WeCroak. It reminds me several times a day that I am going to die. It's not to make me depressed; it's to wake me up so I live my life fully. It helps me reflect on how I could have done things differently in the messy moments, to not sweat the small stuff, and to let go of my grudges and anger every day. And it always creates an interesting talking point when someone sees the notification come up on my phone: 'Don't forget you're going to die.'

This is where the Stoic sentiment of carpe diem or 'seize the day' comes in. First coined by the Roman poet Horace, it can be translated as 'pluck today', grab it with both hands. It was one of the primary philosophies expounded by the Stoics that has stood the test of time. Seneca said:

> Let us therefore set out whole-heartedly, leaving aside our many distractions and exert ourselves in this single purpose, before we realize too late the swift and unstoppable flight of time and are left behind. As each day arises, welcome it as the very best day of all, and make it your own possession. We must seize what flees.

The point is, we remember our death to create a better future for ourselves. We let go of regrets and move forward in a better and lighter way. Death makes life richer. As Socrates said, 'Not life, but good life, is to be chiefly valued.'

YOLO

While popular Canadian rapper Drake may have popularised the acronym YOLO or 'you only live once' in 2011, spreading the carpe diem vibes to a wide audience of this modern generation, it has been around since the ancient philosophers started to put into words the most fundamental teachings. In Buddhism, yoga and mindfulness, the emphasis on being in the present moment is at the heart of their wisdom.

In the *Dhammapada*, the Buddha gives an instruction that is both fierce and compassionate: 'If someone has abused you, beat you, robbed you, abandon your thoughts of anger. Soon you will die. Life is too short to live with hatred.' The teaching invites us to focus on the present moment instead of the past. It's a wake-up call.

The Buddha also says, 'Do not dwell in the past, do not dream of the future, concentrate the mind on the present moment.'

ATHA

The first word of Patanjali's *Yoga Sutras* is 'atha' or now. It is an auspicious word, and some teachers suggest that if you really understand what atha means, you will understand everything and reach enlightenment, or liberation. The word is a call to action, to wake up! Practising mindfulness, as per Jon Kabat-Zinn definition of 'paying attention, on purpose, in the present moment, non-judgementally', is the key to staying in the 'now', no matter what is going on. It is in this spirit that we live every moment of our lives on purpose, using each one as a teacher.

KINSHIP

Aboriginal Elder Aunty Munya tells me it's only when we see everything and everyone as family that we can become kinder and more compassionate – and ultimately forgive. If there was any group of people who would have reason to resent right-wing party leader Pauline Hanson, it would be the Aboriginal and Torres Strait Islander peoples. But Aunty Munya describes how the concept of kinship means that compassion extends everywhere and to everyone:

> Country is everything. Country is all-inclusive. There are kinship systems for everything, for all the animals, all the plants, all the stars, like everything. It's really coming back to that belief, that connection, the things we share as humans. In

Aboriginal languages, there was no word for 'thank you' because there was kinship and reciprocity. There was no need for it was an unnecessary word and I think it's similar to forgiveness ...

You know, I talk about Pauline Hanson. Aunty Pauline Hanson, we call her that, and we'll go, 'Oh, you heard what old Aunty said now the other day? She's going off about it, this and that.' But there's even a great forgiveness in that, that we just think she's a bit 'cartwarra', a bit crazy, but she's valuable. She's part of Australian society.

We always will have one of those relatives that we just think are so far away from us, but kinship brings us back together again ... Their opinions matter. They're not different from us. They are part of us. And so that's the wonderful thing that kinship teaches, is that we're all connected, and there's no divorcing from one another. So there's a sense of surrender for our mob, that it's got nothing to do with me or my ego. It's just the way things are, everyone has a place, everyone belongs, and everyone is family, whether we like it or not. There's wonderful forgiveness that can come with that. What if everyone is family and that they're not strangers?

IT STARTS WITH YOU

When you look at the sum total of your life, there's only one thing that is consistent across it all. Every experience, every relationship, the wins, losses, tragedies and triumphs, mistakes and miracles, they all have one thing in common – you. If you want to make sense of your life, if you genuinely desire more forgiveness, if you want to grow into the best version of yourself, it has to start with you. Self-study, or 'svadhyaya' is at the heart of transforming your life, and it's one of the observances in the *Yoga Sutras*.

We see the process of svadhyaya at the heart of so many great stories and myths. Our hero embarks on a journey to reach some elusive goal. They overcome obstacles and gain self-knowledge thanks to the trials of their journey. Like Arjuna in the Gita, we are constantly on the hero's journey, navigating the battlefield of life. It's our job to stay awake and seek to understand who and what we are through svadhyaya.

Meditation practice is another great way to work with this process. In meditation, we get to observe the monkey mind, jumping around from thought to thought, in all its magnificence. The beauty of this practice is that you become a good observer. Simply by watching your thoughts as they arise and fall, with no story or judgement, you become familiar with the patterns of your own mind. As you become familiar with the nature of your mind, thoughts stop having so much power over you.

CONNECTING WITH THE SACRED

As we moved through the chapters of this book, several times the idea has emerged of connecting to something greater than yourself. This concept is at the heart of many spiritual traditions and practices within them are there in order to feel a connection to that. First we unite with the quieter, deeper part of ourself, and the idea is that from that place, we can connect with something greater. Call it the universe, your personal choice of God, our universal consciousness. I feel connected to it when I jump in the ocean, practise yoga or meditation, or sit with my teachers. I love sacred spaces like churches and temples because they feel elevated, not mundane, consecrated in some way. For some people it's being immersed in nature, prayer or meditation. There's no one way to do it; it is a uniquely personal experience. But if we really want to forgive, if we really want to 'swaha' and offer our suffering up, then we must have a relationship with the sacred.

Aboriginal Elder, Aunty Munya talks about connecting the sacred in this way:

> Yeah, for me, it's about communing with the land, with people, with your environment. Dadirri (deep listening), for me, takes you to the heart of that, where you can open your dreaming ears and eyes, listen to your environment, open up to other worlds, and see things that you don't otherwise see in this material world. Opening up to that which is sacred in the world. If people aren't able to express themselves through words, or whatever, it's listening in another way, having that ability to see the unseen scars and to know the unfelt pain.

RELATIONSHIPS ARE OUR TEACHERS

Seema tells me that our relationships are part of our karma, and when we start to see that they are our teachers, we can be more playful in how we relate. She says:

> A good practice is that once you start realising that we are actually the Supreme Consciousness and all this world is not real. It's just like we are here, we are born here in a certain place, in a certain house, with certain people to forget our, how you say, 'play the game' and get rid of all the past karmas that we have to do with these people. When you are able to see yourself as somebody playing that game, you know, then things get much more clearer and easier to understand. And once you get that third-person view of the world and the surrounding and the situations, it's easier to forgive and forget.

FROM SEEING CRIME TO EXPERIENCING GROWTH

According to TCM, the fire element is the gateway to our higher self, our spiritual virtues of compassion, understanding and deep acceptance. Nature invites us to grow by creating situations and events that stress us in unique ways, allowing us to act in ways that develop virtues of patience, kindness etc. These opportunities are necessary for us to cultivate character and virtue. Most of our essential stresses are caused by the infliction of harm by another. They are simply a vehicle to stress us appropriately so we evolve. Seeing the wisdom and intelligence in this will shift the lens from a crime requiring forgiveness to the limitations of another correctly employed to stimulate growth. As TCM physician Jade Clark says:

> As we grow spiritually, we are far more accepting of people and their limitations and less interested in judging perceived shortcomings when our expectations are unmet. When we understand one's limitations, it is unreasonable to expect anything better from them, let alone judge and condemn them for them.

GRATITUDE FOR THE PEOPLE WHO HELP US GROW

In the great Hindu text *Ramayana*, forgiveness is one of the main themes. A young prince, Shri Ram, the next in line to become king, was betrayed by his father's second wife, Kaikeyi. On the day of his coronation, she decided to make her son king instead. You'd think that being sent away from your rightful place would be enough to make you fight to stay or hate your evil stepmother. But no, Shri

Ram respected her wishes as he would his own mother's and gracefully left with his brother and wife Sita.

When he returned home after fourteen years in exile, he did so without an ounce of hatred in his heart. He didn't punish his stepmother. Instead, he thanked her for all he learned through the process of his banishment. Without it, he said he never would have understood his love for his father, the goodness of his stepbrother who took his place on the throne, the depth of friendship with allies like Hanuman and Sugriv, the purity of his beloved Sita, the power of his enemies, and most importantly, his own strength. He was grateful rather than hateful, choosing peace for those around him.

MEMENTO MORI: A SUMMARY

- Recognising our impermanence helps us prioritise what truly matters in life.
- Contemplating death encourages us to live each day as if it were our last, freeing us from distractions.
- Kinship in Indigenous culture reminds us of how connected we all are.
- Regularly examining our lives helps us acknowledge mistakes and grow from them, creating space for

personal transformation.

- Teachings from various philosophical traditions stress the importance of focusing on the present moment rather than the past or future.
- Life's difficulties serve as valuable lessons, guiding us towards growth and deeper understanding.
- Accepting both the good and bad in life is essential.

CONNECTING TO THE SACRED

For each one of us, the means to connecting to the sacred will be different. Start to notice those moments you feel connected to something beyond the mundane. Perhaps it's walking at sunrise, listening to music, or watching your baby laugh. Pay attention so you can consciously bring more of that relationship with the sacred into your life. In the exercise below, however, we will take a moment of mindfulness while in savasana, or corpse pose, to foster that connection. Corpse pose is often placed at the end of yoga class, not only to relax after moving and breathing, but to practise our death in a state of consciousness and surrender.

EXERCISE

Lie on your back, arms either side of your body, palms facing up, feet hip width or wider. Scan the body and completely relax, sensing the ground beneath you. Feel how sensations come and go, impermanent, always changing. Observe your breath and slowly breathe in, and out. Return to breathing naturally. Listen to the sounds, smell, taste. Watch how your thoughts are jumping around and making meaning of this experience, putting it through some kind of filter. Now see if you can get curious about that part of you observing all of that. That part of you that animates your breath, that experiences all you do, that deeper part of you. Feel how that part is connected to all things. Can you feel the thread between you and everything? You and something vast, something greater than yourself. Something sacred. No separation between you and it. When you are ready, set your hands in a shape of gratitude, and chant om. Then listen to the silence that follows.

EPILOGUE: A PROMISING FUTURE

Maya Angelou, born in 1928 as Marguerite Annie Johnson, was one of the greatest American poets, authors, civil rights activists and storytellers of our time. But her humble beginnings were fraught with trauma and abuse. From the age of eight, she was mute for five years after reporting her abuser, who was charged and subsequently murdered (most likely by one of her family members). Throughout her life, she worked as a cook, streetcar conductor, waitress, singer, dancer, editor, teacher, civil rights organiser and actress before becoming one of America's most celebrated writers. She spoke often and passionately about the need to forgive everyone, and look for the sameness in all of us rather than the difference:

> We cannot change the past, but we can change our attitude toward it. Uproot guilt and plant forgiveness. Tear out arrogance and seed humility. Exchange love for hate – thereby, making the present comfortable and the future promising.

A FICTIONAL ENDING – HOPE

Bigambul and Wakka woman Melanie Saward wrote *Burn,* one of my favourite reads last year. It is a powerful novel about prejudice, explored through Andrew, a young Indigenous boy living in Tasmania.

When I spoke to Melanie, she told me there wasn't a lot of forgiveness in the text when she was writing it, and because of that, it wasn't working. Something felt off – until it landed with her publisher and they discussed the possibility of making it hopeful. It was this word, 'hope', that she carried through the process.

She was inspired by a speech by writer Melissa Lukashenko, delivered in 2017 to the First Nations Australia Writers Network. It had been published on Meanjin, and in it, Lukashenko talked about writing as a sovereign act and how there is power in all kinds of stories. Melanie says: 'Her characters always possessed beauty, humour, power and a connection to land. And I really took this on board, along with this idea of – I really want to give hope. And I didn't want to perpetuate negative stereotypes about my people.'

Fiction is a powerful vehicle for empathy, and Melanie realised she had written the story with a sad ending because that's the reality. 'But to put hope in, I could use fiction. The fiction ending is the powerful ending, right? Because it shows kids we love them, and that we understand them and that trauma is inherited, and that the things that they do aren't always their fault. And I think that there is forgiveness in that. That we have to let kids be a clean slate.'

ADAM GOODES – THE LIVING EMBODIMENT OF FORGIVENESS

Adam Roy Goodes is an Adnyamathanha man who has stood at the intersection of greatness and adversity. A former professional Australian rules footballer for the Sydney Swans in the AFL, Adam's list of achievements reads like the stuff of legend: dual Brownlow Medallist, dual premiership player, four-time All-Australian, a proud member of the Indigenous Team of the Century, and even a representative for Australia in the International Rules Series.

But beyond the accolades and the on-field brilliance, it's

the heart of Adam Goodes that truly sets him apart. His work in the community and his tireless advocacy against racism earned him the honour of being named Australian of the Year in 2014. His pride in his culture and his efforts to empower Aboriginal and Torres Strait Islander communities have made him not just a leader in sport but a powerful voice for equality and justice in Australia.

In 2013, Adam found himself at the centre of one of the most contentious and painful chapters in Australian sport. His decision to speak openly and courageously about racism made him the target of a relentless booing campaign by opposition fans. Week after week, stadiums echoed with the jeers, a stark reminder of the deep-seated issues Australia continues to face regarding race and identity.

The toll was immense. Adam, a man who had given everything to his sport and his country, took indefinite leave from the game in 2015, eventually retiring at the end of that season. His departure marked not just the end of a football career but the beginning of a national conversation. The 'booing saga' sparked a debate about the nature of racism in Australia, forcing the nation to confront uncomfortable truths. In 2019, two powerful documentaries, *The Final Quarter* and *The Australian Dream*, captured the emotional and cultural impact of Adam's experience, bringing his story to screens across the world. The AFL, in that same year, issued a formal apology for not doing more to protect him from the abuse he endured.

If there was ever anyone well placed to speak about forgiveness, it's Adam Goodes. His story is one of forgiveness at the deepest level, both of himself and others. Through the relentless booing, the hostility and the personal cost, Adam stood strong, not only advocating for change but also learning how to let go of the bitterness that could easily have consumed him.

I first met Adam in the make-up room at the ABC when I was rehearsing for *Play School* and he was in shooting a little segment for the show. It takes a lot to make me blush, but so great is my respect for this man that I went mute and couldn't talk. Determined not to do the same when he agreed to talk to me for this book, I did lots of preparation and took some deep breaths before jumping on our Zoom call, where I had the privilege of hearing him talk about forgiveness. It has shaped his life, leadership and relationships.

He starts our chat by sharing a pivotal moment he experienced during a twelve-week meditation course with leadership mentor Tammy Roos. During one of the sessions, Tammy handed him a piece of cardboard with a handwritten message that would have a lifelong impact on him:

> She handed me this little piece of cardboard and said, 'I keep getting this message for you: I am able to forgive.' I remember looking at it and thinking, 'What does this mean for me?' Then, it really hit me because at that time in my life, I wasn't sure if I could forgive myself for a lot of things.

That simple, handwritten note was profound for Adam, who had been grappling with guilt over a major decision he made when he was seventeen, leaving his family behind in Melbourne to pursue a rugby career in Sydney. He said, 'I grew up in a single-parent household. My mum raised me and my two younger brothers, and I always felt this huge responsibility to take care of them. When I left for Sydney, I felt like I was abandoning them. That guilt stayed with me for years.'

For Adam, that note from Tammy became more than just a message, it became a daily reminder:

> I've kept that piece of cardboard with me everywhere. Sometimes it's in my locker at the football club, or I'll come across it in a drawer at home. Every time I see it, it reminds me of the importance of forgiving myself. It's a reminder that I'm allowed to make mistakes and let them go.

He talks about forgiving himself, emphasising that it wasn't an easy process, particularly when it came to his family:

> Forgiving myself for leaving them was one of the hardest things I've ever had to do. I used to think, 'I'm a bad son, a bad brother because I wasn't there for them when they needed me.' But over time, I realised that leaving wasn't about abandoning them, it was about doing something for myself, something I needed to do. And that's okay.

He circles back many times to his 'why', and how it's at the centre of everything he does. It's holding on to who you are, your purpose, as the Stoics suggest. And the idea we saw in yoga, of giving something up to get something else. He says:

> Whenever I start doubting myself or getting too hard on myself, I always ask, 'Why am I doing this?' It always comes back to my family and the need to create a better life for them and for myself. That's the driving force behind every sacrifice I've made. Reminding myself of my 'why' helps me forgive myself for the tough choices and the time I've spent away from them.

Adam also speaks about how letting things go and focusing on the present and future has helped him move forward. He says:

> After every game, whether we won or lost, I didn't want to sit and dwell on it for too long. There's always a review, but by Monday night, that's in the past. I'm always looking forward ... how can I improve, what can I do better, and how can I help the team move forward? Forgiveness is about that too ... it's not just about the past, it's about how you move forward and focus on what's next.

He focuses on using his energy for more important

things instead of beating himself up or ruminating:

> Once I learned to forgive myself, everything changed. It was like carrying around this weight for so long, and suddenly, I didn't have to anymore. I stopped holding onto things that didn't serve me – guilt, shame, resentment. It created space for more important things, like being present with my family and showing up as a better leader.

He says self-forgiveness fosters compassion, which allows for people to mess up, make mistakes and be imperfect. And ultimately it frees us, we become lighter:

> Forgiveness is such a powerful thing. You have to be able to forgive yourself before you can truly forgive anyone else. People make mistakes. I've made plenty of them. But if you hold onto every little thing, it just builds up and weighs you down. Life is too short to be walking around carrying all that.

He touches on what we looked at in the Stoics' memento mori concept, stressing the importance of staying present and remembering that life is fleeting.

> We don't have much time in this life. We're all going to die one day, and I think we forget that. We get caught up in all these small things that don't really matter. When you remind yourself of that ... of how short life is ... it becomes easier to let go of grudges, guilt and anger. None of it is worth holding onto when you realise how little time we actually have.

And like Peter Gould's story of the enlightened man going to sleep each night with no grudges, Adam talks about forgiveness being a daily practice:

> Forgiveness isn't something you do once and then move on. It's something you practise every single day. Sometimes it's the small things – maybe I didn't handle a situation as well as I could have. Other times it's bigger things. But it's always a practice.

Adam also draws inspiration from his mother, who always practised forgiveness, no matter what hardships she faced, and how forgiveness lets us off the hook, not others.

Now, as a father, Adam tries to instil the same values in his children: 'I tell my kids all the time, "Don't be afraid to make mistakes. When you mess up, apologise, forgive yourself, and move on." Life is too short to be weighed down by guilt or anger. I want them to understand that forgiveness is the key to living fully.'

Adam tells me when we are in the midst of dark times, and he has faced many, there's a few things he's found helpful. He remembers we cannot control everything. He remembers his 'why' – his purpose. He uses those experiences to grow and find gratitude: 'It helped me face adversity. It teaches me discipline. It makes me stronger. It makes me appreciate the friends I have, the life I'm living.'

And he believes that there are always silver linings. 'So for me, those darkest periods in my life, I couldn't see it at the time, but there was always a positive element to come from it. And I think we can always look back at the darkest periods, there's always a silver lining. I lost my mum two and a bit years ago. And even in my mother's death at sixty-two, you know, it was incredibly sad, but there's so much positivity out of reflecting on her life. What she's left behind, how she'll always be with us. So many lessons learned from that very strong, determined woman.'

This conversation not only brings all the threads together for me, but Adam's comment about his mum hits home particularly hard. At the end of our chat, when I'm thanking him for his time, he says: 'You know, I just think of my mum, how she raised three boys, and the incredible job that she did. So I'm sure you're doing an equally good job with your little one, Rachael.'

I think, 'No, Adam, I'm not doing an incredible job, I feel like I'm failing at all the things all the time.' And I realise maybe that's my work, that's where my forgiveness lies. To forgive myself for the imperfect moments and every bad choice I've made, knowing there will be many more. To fully embrace the one messy life I have, not the one I didn't get to live. To see forgiveness as a lifelong journey rather than a destination. To do my best, to stay awake, to be kind, to let go of whatever is no longer serving me, to show up in each moment, be accountable when I miss the mark and learn what I can from the mayhem. Maybe that's enough.

~

As we come to the end of this journey through these pages together, I hope you feel it too, that forgiveness is not some ultimate destination. It's not a place we get to on the top of the mountain, looking down on everyone and everything else. It is a process, a way of being in the world, an imperfect practice we can stay engaged in for the rest of our lives.

Hopefully you got some insight from those who shared their stories of how they managed to forgive, sometimes the unforgivable. That you see there is no one way of doing it, that ultimately, creativity is the key. Whether it's ocean swims and body surfing or carrying secret bits of paper in our pockets to remind us of what is so easy to forget. Letting go, perhaps with boundaries in place, giving, or giving up something we really don't want to. Maybe curiosity, compassion and empathy resonated, or, as Drakey says, you just going straight to mercy. We could remember we're going to die, or that we all make mistakes or get clear on our 'why' or purpose.

From the conversations with so many different people around their perspectives and ideas of what forgiveness entails, we can see that there are some differences, yes, but many threads that bind them. We reflected on the yogic understanding that everything is just energy moving through form, and this connects us all. And just as we cannot separate the mind, body and energy from one another, we can be separate from one another. How we are in the world impacts one another.

Maybe the promising future Maya Angelou talks about is exactly that. Remembering we are all in it together and embracing each messy moment. And yes, the world feels like a dark, complicated and very uncertain place right now. And yes, there is too much suffering, and it hurts me to my bones. The polarisation and division are hurting us all on a personal, micro and global scale. And yes, I also think we have so much work to do.

But look how far we have all come despite it all. I'm not that broken single mum with a newborn. I'm grateful for Gabe's dad and the bridges we've built. We are making progress in reconciliation on the national stage. We've come through darker ages of history than the ones we find ourselves in now.

And just as Adam Goodes attested to, after every dark period, there has been an age of enlightenment, a calm after the storm. How, no matter what, they always seem to appear. So perhaps that's what we all need to do. Do our best. Follow the advice the incredible voices within these pages have shared. And have faith in the silver linings. Or perhaps, together, we can dream up our own. A silver lining for humanity, a kinder, more compassionate and forgiving world. And like Nasim does with her art, and Matt does with his film, and Simi does with her writing, and Adam does with his story, and Mel does with her works of fiction, we can rewrite our own promising future.

Maybe fiction is the answer, each one of us imagining a new narrative for ourselves. The art of forgiveness starts with a dream. As Martin Luther King once said: 'I say to you today, my friends, that in spite of the difficulties and frustrations of the moment, I still have a dream.' Stay creative, stay curious. After all, there is no wisdom in the answers, just the questions.

BIBLIOGRAPHY

- Bachelard, Michael, 'A new Australian baby born in squalor in a Syrian detention camp', *The Sydney Morning Herald*, 10 December 2019, https://www.smh.com.au/world/middle-east/a-new-australian-baby-born-in-squalor-in-a-syrian-detention-camp-20191210-p53ioi.html
- P 18 "Differing structural brain anatomy suggests that forgiveness could be a trait people are born with." Moawad, Heidi, MD, 'The Neurobiology of Forgiveness', *NeurologyLive,* 25 September 2018, https://www.neurologylive.com/view/neurobiology-forgiveness
- P 18 "His research found that some people are naturally more forgiving, and those who are, have higher levels of agreeableness and lower levels of neuroticism." Weir Kirsten, 'Forgiveness can improve mental and physical health', *American Psychological Association (APA),* January 2017, https://www.apa.org/monitor/2017/01/ce-corner
- P 18 "They tend to be more satisfied with their lives and have less depression, anxiety, stress, anger and hostility", *Hopkins Medicine*, 'Forgiveness: Your Health Depends on it.' https://

www.hopkinsmedicine.org/health/wellness-and-prevention/forgiveness-your-health-depends-on-it#definitions_block

- P 18 "Differences in metabolic brain activity associated with the inclination to forgive may mean that this trait could be altered throughout life." Moawad, Heidi, MD, 'The Neurobiology of Forgiveness', *NeurologyLive,* 25 September 2018, https://www.neurologylive.com/view/neurobiology-forgiveness
- P 20 "It's akin to lab rats in a cage, pressing a lever over and over to get a drink, but instead of receiving sugar water, they receive a toxic substance", Webster, Corey, 'The Power of Forgiveness According to Neuroscience', *Medium,* 27 August 2018, https://medium.com/@cwebster_32318/the-power-of-forgiveness-according-to-neuroscience-dc19fa2a2ef7
- P 20 "A study by Yoav Litvin and colleagues from Donald Pfaff's Laboratory of Neurobiology and Behavior at Rockerfeller University illustrated ..." Litvin, Yoav, Gen Murakami, Donald W Pfaff, 'Effects of chronic social defeat on behavioral and neural correlates of sociality: Vasopressin, oxytocin and the vasopressinergic V1b receptor', *Science Direct,* 1 June 2011, https://www.sciencedirect.com/science/article/abs/pii/S0031938411001247
- P 20 "When the hypothalamus triggers the fight-or-flight state", LeWine, Howard, 'Understanding the stress response', *Harvard Health Publishing*, 3 April 2024, https://www.health.harvard.edu/staying-healthy/understanding-the-stress-response
- P 21 "The American Psychological Association says that repeated, long-term activation of the fight-or-flight response ...", Shaw, William PhD, Susan Labott-Smith, PhD, ABPP, Matthew M.

Burg, PhD, Camelia Hostinar, PhD, Nicholas Alen, BA, Miranda AL van Tilburg, PhD, Gary G Berntson, PhD, Steven M Tovian, PhD, ABPP, FAClinP, FAClinHP and Malina Spirito, PsyD, Med, 'Stress effects on the body', *American Psychological Association,* 1 November 2018, https://www.apa.org/topics/stress/body

- P 21 "Consultant psychiatrist Sami Ouanes and psychiatrist and professor for geriatric psychiatry, Julius Popp …" Ounes, Sami and Julius Popp, 'High Cortisol and the Risk of Dementia and Alzheimer's Disease: A Review of the Literature', *Frontiers,* 1 March 2019, https://www.frontiersin.org/journals/aging-neuroscience/articles/10.3389/fnagi.2019.00043/full
- P 21 'Post-traumatic stress disorder as a risk factor for dementia: systematic review and meta-analysis', Cambridge University Press, 15 September 2020, https://www.cambridge.org/core/journals/the-british-journal-of-psychiatry/article/posttraumatic-stress-disorder-as-a-risk-factor-for-dementia-systematic-review-and-metaanalysis/2C7CB7708472ADAE1484C8E658D8F892
- P21 Echouffo-Tcheugui, Justin B, Sarah C Conner, Jayandra J Himali, Pauline Maillard, Charles S DeCarli, Alexa S Beiser, Ramachandran S Vasan, Sudha Seshadri, 'Circulating cortisol and cognitive and structural brain measures', *National Library of Medicine* 20 November 2018, https://pmc.ncbi.nlm.nih.gov/articles/PMC6260201/
- P 21 Mariotti, Agnese, 'The effects of chronic stress on health: new insights into the molecular mechanisms of brain–body communication', *National Library of Medicine,* 1 November 2015, https://pmc.ncbi.nlm.nih.gov/articles/PMC5137920/
- P 24 David R Williams, Everett Worthington, Loren Toussaint,

Forgiveness and Health, Springer, Dordrecht, 2015

- P 24 Weir Kirsten, 'Forgiveness can improve mental and physical health', *American Psychological Association (APA),* January 2017, https://www.apa.org/monitor/2017/01/ce-corner
- P 24 Van Oyen Witvliet, C, T E Ludwig, & K L Vander Laan, 2001, 'Granting forgiveness or harboring grudges: implications for emotion, physiology, and health', *National Library of Medicine*, 12 March 2001, https://pubmed.ncbi.nlm.nih.gov/11340919/
- P 27 Anna Freud, *The Ego and the Mechanisms of Defence (revised edition)*, Karnac Books, London, 1993, https://www.sas.upenn.edu/~cavitch/pdf-library/Anna_Freud_Ego_chs_3_4_5.pdf
- P 28 Ivan Nyklicek, Lydia Temoshok and Ad Vingerhoets, '*Emotional Expression and Health*', Brunner-Routledge, East Sussex, 2004
- P 28 Roberts, Nicole A, Robert W Levenson, James J Gross, 'Cardiovascular costs of emotion suppression cross ethnic lines', *Science Direct,* October 2008, https://www.sciencedirect.com/science/article/abs/pii/S0167876008007009?via%3Dihub
- P 28 Beblo, Thomas, Silvia Fernando, Sabrina Klocke, Julia Griepenstroh, Steffen Aschenbrenner, Martin Driessen, 'Increased suppression of negative and positive emotions in major depression', *Science Direct,* 10 December 2012, https://pmc.ncbi.nlm.nih.gov/articles/PMC3939772/
- P 28 Chapman, Benjamin P, Kevin Fiscella, Ichiro Kawachi, Paul Duberstein, Peter Muennig, 'Emotion suppression and mortality risk over a 12-year follow-up', *Science Direct,* October 2013, https://www.sciencedirect.com/science/article/abs/pii/S0022399913003036

- P 30 Anaïs Nin, *Seduction of the Minotaur*, Swallow Press, 1961
- P 37 Yamamoto, Kyoko, Masanori Kimura, Miki, Osaka, 'Sorry, Not Sorry: Effects of Different Types of Apologies and Self-Monitoring on Non-verbal Behaviors', *National Library of Medicine,* 26 August 2021, https://pmc.ncbi.nlm.nih.gov/articles/PMC8428520/#:~:text
- P 37 Strang, Sabrina, Verena Utikal, Urs Fischbacher, Bernd Weber, Armin Falk, 'Neural Correlates of Receiving an Apology and Active Forgiveness: An fMRI Study', *National Library of Medicine,* 5 February 2014, https://pmc.ncbi.nlm.nih.gov/articles/PMC3914861/
- P 37 Beverly Engel, *The Power of Apology,* John Wiley & Sons Inc, New York, 2001
- P 37 Leunissen, Joost M, David De Cremer, Marius van Dijke, Christopher P Reinders Folmer, 'Forecasting Errors in the Averseness of Apologising.' 2014. https://eprints.soton.ac.uk/367348/1/Leunissen%2520et%2520al%25202014%2520Forecasting%2520errors%2520in%2520apologizing.pdf
- P 37 Takaku, Seiji, Bernard Weiner, Ken-Ichi Ohbuchi. 'A cross-cultural examination of the effects of apology and perspective taking on forgiveness', *Journal of Language and Social Psychology,* March 2001, https://www.researchgate.net/publication/247743410_A_Cross-Cultural_Examination_of_the_Effects_of_Apology_and_Perspective_Taking_on_Forgiveness
- P 58 Tastanova, Aigerim, Donah Henrikson, Mariya Mun, Nadiya Akhtayeva, 'The relationship between creativity and yoga nidra as a mindfulness practice: Considering the possibilities for

wellbeing and education', *Science Direct,* June 2024, https://www.sciencedirect.com/science/article/abs/pii/S1871187124000385

- P 58 Pandi-Perumal, Seithikupippu R, David Warren Spence, Neena Srivastava, Divya Kanchibhotla, Kamakhya Kumar, Gaurav Saurabh Sharma, Ravi Gupta, Gitanjali Batmanabane, *National Library of Medicine,* 23 April 2023, https://pmc.ncbi.nlm.nih.gov/articles/PMC9033521/#Sec12
- P 63 Chödrön, Pema, 'Pema Chödrön on Waking Up – and Benefiting Others', *Lion's Roar,* 25 February 2017, https://www.lionsroar.com/no-time-to-lose/
- P 70 Chödrön, Pema, *Don't Bite the Hook,* Shambala Publications, 2007
- P 73 Chödrön, Pema, 'Take Three Conscious Breaths', *Lion's Roar,* 2 April 2017, https://www.lionsroar.com/take-three-conscious-breaths/
- P 73 Tan, Chade-Meng, 'Just 6 seconds of Mindfulness Can Make You More Effective', *Harvard Business Review,* 30 December 2015, https://hbr.org/2015/12/just-6-seconds-of-mindfulness-can-make-you-more-effective
- P 75 Weir Kirsten, 'Forgiveness can improve mental and physical health', *American Psychological Association (APA),* January 2017, https://www.apa.org/monitor/2017/01/ce-corner
- P 76 Wargo, Eric, 'How Many Seconds to a First Impression?', *Psychological Science,* 1 July 2006, https://www.psychologicalscience.org/observer/how-many-seconds-to-a-first-impression
- P 82 Chu, Brianna, Komal Marwaha, Terrence Sanvictores, Ayoola O Awosika, Derek Ayers, 'Physiology, Stress Reaction', *National Library of Medicine,* updated May 2024, https://www.

ncbi.nlm.nih.gov/books/NBK541120/

- P 82 'Australia's Children', Australian Institute of Health and Welfare, 2020, https://www.aihw.gov.au/reports/children-youth/australias-children/contents/justice-safety/bullying
- P 100 Epiticus, Sharon Lebell, *Art of Living: The Classical Manual on Virtue, Happiness, and Effectiveness,* HarperOne, 26 June 2007
- P 104 Education resources on sound at *Science World,* https://www.scienceworld.ca/resource/sound/#:~:text
- P 105 Goldsby, Tamara, Michale E Goldsby, Mary McWalters, Paul J Mills, 'Effects of Singing Bowl Sound Meditation on Mood, Tension, and Well-being: An Observational Study', *National Library of Medicine,* 30 September 2016.
- P 108 Lin, Jue, Elissa Epel, 'Stress and telomere shortening: Insights from cellular mechanisms', *National Library of Medicine,* 1 November 2021, https://pmc.ncbi.nlm.nih.gov/articles/PMC8920518/
- P 111 Davey, Steven, Jasmin Halberstadt and Elliot Bell, 'Where is emotional feeling felt in the body? An integrative review,' *PLOS*, 22 December 2021, https://journals.plos.org/plosone/article?id=10.1371/journal.pone.0261685
- P 111 West, Jennifer, Belle Liang, Joseph Spinazzola, 'Trauma Sensitive Yoga as a complementary treatment for posttraumatic stress disorder: A Qualitative Descriptive analysis', *National Library of Medicine,* 4 July 2016, https://pmc.ncbi.nlm.nih.gov/articles/PMC5404814/
- P 112 Shapiro, Francine, 'The Role of Eye Movement Desensitization and Reprocessing (EMDR) Therapy in Medicine:

Addressing the Psychological and Physical Symptoms Stemming from Adverse Life Experiences', *National Library of Medicine,* 2014, https://pmc.ncbi.nlm.nih.gov/articles/PMC3951033/

- P 112 Bach, Donna, Gary Groesbeck, Peter Stapleton, Rebecca Sims, Katharina Blickheuser, Dawson Church, 'Clinical EFT (Emotional Freedom Techniques) Improves Multiple Physiological Markers of Health', *National Library of Medicine,* 19 February 2019, https://pmc.ncbi.nlm.nih.gov/articles/PMC6381429/
- P 113 Gracanin, Asmir, Lauren M Bylsma, Ad J J M Vingerhoets, 'Is crying a self-soothing behavior?', *National Library of Medicine,* 28 May 2014, https://pmc.ncbi.nlm.nih.gov/articles/PMC4035568/
- P 114 Fredrickson, Barbara L, Bethany E Kok, 'Upward spirals of the heart: autonomic flexibility, as indexed by vagal tone, reciprocally and prospectively predicts positive emotions and social connectedness', *National Library of Medicine,* December 2010, https://pubmed.ncbi.nlm.nih.gov/20851735/
- P 115 Kok, Bethany, Kimberly A Coffey, Michael A Cohn, Lahnna I Catalino, Tanya Vacharkulksemsuk, Sara B Algoe, Mary Brantley, Barbara L Fredrickson, 'How positive emotions build physical health: perceived positive social connections account for the upward spiral between positive emotions and vagal tone', *National Library of Medicine,* 6 May 2013, https://pubmed.ncbi.nlm.nih.gov/23649562/
- P 115 Wolkin, Jennifer, 'How the Brain Changes When You Meditate', *Mindful,* August 2015, https://www.mindful.org/how-the-brain-changes-when-you-meditate/
- P 116 'Stress relief from laughter? It's no joke', *Mayo Clinic,*

September 2023, https://www.mayoclinic.org/healthy-lifestyle/stress-management/in-depth/stress-relief/art-20044456

- P 117 Lichtenfeld, Stephanie, Markus A Maier, Vanessa L Buechner, Maria Fernandez Capo, 'The Influence of Decisional and Emotional Forgiveness on Attributions', *National Library of Medicine,* 25 June 2019, https://pmc.ncbi.nlm.nih.gov/articles/PMC6603330/
- P 118 'What is Cognitive Behavioural Therapy?', *American Psychological Association, 2017,* https://www.apa.org/ptsd-guideline/patients-and-families/cognitive-behavioral
- P 119 Swami Mukundananda, translation of *The Bhagavad Gita* 6:9, https://www.holy-bhagavad-gita.org/chapter/6/verse/9
- P 122 June Price, Tangney, 'Interview With June Price Tangney About *Shame in the Therapy Hour*', *American Psychological Association*, APA Convention transcript, 2011, https://www.apa.org/pubs/books/interviews/4317264-tangney#:~:text
- P 125 Saffrey, Collen, Amy Summerville, Neal Roese, 'Praise for regret: People value regret above other negative emotions', *National Library of Medicine,* 5 June 2008, https://pmc.ncbi.nlm.nih.gov/articles/PMC2413060/
- P 125 'Inability to shake regrets can have effects on physical health', *Science Daily,* March 2011, https://www.sciencedaily.com/releases/2011/03/110301111503.htm
- P 125 Davidai, Shai, Thomas Gilovich, 'The ideal road not taken: the self-discrepancies involved in people's most enduring regrets', *American Psychological Association,* 2018, https://psycnet.apa.org/record/2017-21180-001?doi=1
- P 126 Busch, Holger, Jan Hofer, Iva Polackova Solcova, Peter

Tavel, 'Generativity affects fear of death through ego integrity in German, Czech, and Cameroonian older adults', *Science Direct,* July–August 2018, https://www.sciencedirect.com/science/article/abs/pii/S0167494318300633

- P 127 Dr Bullock, Grace, 'New Research on Mindfulness and Forgiveness', *Mindful,* 18 April 2019, https://www.mindful.org/mindful-people-may-be-more-willing-to-forgive/
- P 128 Curran, Thomas and Andrew P Hill, 'Perfectionism Is Increasing Over Time: A Meta-Analysis of Birth Cohort Differences From 1989 to 2016', *American Psychological Association Psychological Bulletin,* 2019, Vol. 145, No.4, 410–429, https://www.apa.org/pubs/journals/releases/bul-bul0000138.pdf
- P 132 Traversa, Marissa, Ying Tan, Stephen C Wright, 'Cancel culture can be collectively validating for groups experiencing harm', *Frontiers in Psychology,* 20 July 2023, https://www.frontiersin.org/journals/psychology/articles/10.3389/fpsyg.2023.1181872/full
- P 132 Jonsson, Linda, 'Cancelling' cancel culture? A study on the impacts of cancel culture on freedom of speech and journalism', Masters Thesis for Södertörn University | School of Social Science, https://www.diva-portal.org/smash/get/diva2:1692723/FULLTEXT02

Acknowledgements

During the pandemic lockdown, I wrote an article on yoga and forgiveness, which felt like a rabbit hole worthy of going deeper into one day. So when my wonderful publisher Kelly Doust approached me a short time later floating the idea of a book on forgiveness, it felt like fate. I naively opened Pandora's box and began walking (some days crawling) the seemingly infinite terrain of forgiveness, knowing these pages could never really contain it, try as I may.

In the Greek myth, the first woman created by the gods, Pandora, is given a container by Zeus and cautioned not to open it. Of course, curiosity gets the better of her and she does, unleashing all the miseries experienced by humankind. But in addition to all the darkness it contains, the box also holds one of the most powerful gifts we can receive – hope.

What was meant to be a simple, pragmatic exploration of forgiveness from an etymology and mindfulness perspective turned into an enormous amount of research, soul-searching and some of the most enriching conversations of my life. Through it all, there has been this overarching theme of hope, which I think I had lost, like so many others, in the blurry post-2019 years.

It is impossible to put into words the immense respect and gratitude I have for the voices within these pages. Their humility, raw honesty and bravery in sharing their stories and perspectives was something to witness. Each contributor humbled and inspired me, and I will forever be indebted, floored by their generosity and vulnerability.

I am profoundly grateful to Kelly Doust and the team at Affirm, for their trust, belief and support. Especially editor Elizabeth Robinson-Griffith and Gabriella Sterio for her excellent copyediting.

To my beloved family and friends who endure the hibernating, unhinged version of me when writing a book on top of single parenting, winter sickness, working full time, touring and making television (after saying each time that I won't write another book until Gabe leaves school) – I love you, don't give up on me.

Special thanks to MZ who checked in on me daily, and kept me from completely unravelling, especially towards the spicy end. And Jordanna, there is no way I would have written this one, (or the first two), without your counsel, guidance and humour.

Most importantly, the biggest gratitude goes to Gabe. He sees me at my best and my worst, always, but especially in these moments. After reading the first chapter, he gave me some pretty brutal feedback. Kelly later gave me exactly the same notes. Thank you for being my favourite person and forgiving me for my imperfect parenting. You, above everyone else, teach me daily the art of forgiveness. I love you the most. x